Praise for
Cracking the *Boy Code*

Adam Cox unpacks in simple language the intricacies of communicating with boys. As a teacher of boys I learnt from every page – the
book is an educational revelation resulting from remarkable face to face
research, and provides an exceptional tool to help parents and teachers
understand what makes boys tick.

—David Anderson B.A, Dip TG, B.Ed, Cert. of Care,
Sydney Australia IBSC Jarvis/Hawley Award Baltimore USA 2017

Cracking the Boy Code offers a thoughtful, accessible guide to developing meaningful communication with the boys in our lives. Adam Cox's
insights, grounded in practical wisdom cultivated over decades of clinical work with boys, provide readers with compelling possibilities for
using non-verbal cues, tone of voice, hands-on activity, and empathetic
listening to connect with boys in a manner both deep and enduring.
Above all, *Cracking the Boy Code* recognizes that boys have a lot on their
minds, and urges all of us to take them seriously as potential partners in
dialogue. Dr. Cox's latest work is both inspiring and instructive.

—Dr. John M. Botti, Head of School, The Browning School

Adam Cox's *Cracking the Boy Code* will become a go to resource for parents, caregivers, teachers and professionals. His deep understanding of
boys and how to provide what they need from the adults in their lives,
is reflected in each chapter with positive, sage advice and strategies. The
real benefactors of this book will be boys, who have adults in their lives
who read this book!

—Mary Gauthier: Executive Director, Greenwood Centre for
Teaching and Learning, Greenwood College School, Toronto

Adam Cox is surely the most important and original writer today on raising boys to be good men. *Cracking the Boy Code* is full of wisdom about the way boys communicate, think and relate. This is a powerful guide for parents, educators and counselors who strive to help boys be their best selves.

—Bradley Adams is the past Executive Director of the International Boys' Schools Coalition and is now an educational consultant.

Cracking
the Boy Code

[HOW TO UNDERSTAND
AND TALK WITH BOYS]

Adam J. Cox, PhD

new society
PUBLISHERS

Cover design by Diane McIntosh.
Cover image: © iStock (621379294)
Text box background: © adobeStock (75003007)
Printed in Canada. First printing April 2018.

Inquiries regarding requests to reprint all or part of *Cracking the Boy Code* should be addressed to New Society Publishers at the address below. To order directly from the publishers, please call toll-free (North America) 1-800-567-6772, or order online at www.newsociety.com

Any other inquiries can be directed by mail to:
New Society Publishers
P.O. Box 189, Gabriola Island, BC V0R 1X0, Canada
(250) 247-9737

LIBRARY AND ARCHIVES CANADA CATALOGUING IN PUBLICATION

Cox, Adam J., author
    Cracking the boy code : how to understand and talk with boys / Adam J. Cox, PhD.

Includes index.
Issued in print and electronic formats.
ISBN 978-0-86571-876-0 (softcover).--ISBN 978-1-55092-669-9 (PDF).--
ISBN 978-1-77142-264-2 (EPUB)
    1. Boys. 2. Child rearing. 3. Communication in families. I. Title.
HQ775.C69 2018   649'.132   C2017-907591-8
                                      C2017-907592-6

New Society Publishers' mission is to publish books that contribute in fundamental ways to building an ecologically sustainable and just society, and to do so with the least possible impact on the environment, in a manner that models this vision.

Contents

Prologue

THIS IS A BOOK ABOUT RELATING TO AND TALKING with boys. I've written this book for you. If you have gotten only this far, I know you must share my concerns. For most of my 20 years as a psychologist, the social and emotional development of boys — how to help boys become capable and confident young men — has been a primary interest. *Cracking the Boy Code* is also a lens for looking at boyhood itself; it makes little sense to suggest how to connect more effectively with boys without also saying something about their psychology.

Some people believe that boys have already been the subject of too much writing. I strongly disagree. Otherwise, we are accepting a discussion of boys' "behavior problems" as all we need to know about who boys are as people. There is so much more to the psychology of boys than behavioral challenges, and that psychology is much more interesting than you might expect.

The way into this story — the most illuminating way to know boys — is to talk with them. The pages that follow may challenge you to relate to someone who may be different than you. And so, *Cracking the Boy Code* is also about life: how different members of a family coexist, get along, and love each other. Compassion and respect for young people is the nitro fuel that gives all the suggestions in this book a chance to work.

You may be encountering the challenge of communicating with boys for the first time. Or perhaps you've been communicating with mixed success for a long time. That was me, some years ago. Almost as soon as I was licensed to practice psychology, people in my community urged me to work with school-age boys. As I am a male therapist, perhaps this was inevitable. Some were emphatic that boys' issues were an important area of need, and that there'd be no shortage of clients in my fledgling counseling practice. I'd already worked with noncommunicative men in different settings: with hardened combat veterans at a US Veterans Administration clinic, visual artists more comfortable sharing images than words at a college counseling center, and very disabled inpatients at a psychiatric hospital. Seeing the need in my community, I accepted the challenge of building a practice around the social and emotional needs of boys, and especially their difficulties with communication. How hard could it be? Well, it was much harder than I thought, and also more rewarding.

My first book, *Boys of Few Words*, was about this work and the difficulties faced by different types of boys (shy, angry, or with learning disabilities).[1] In *Cracking the Boy Code*, I want to describe our challenges in communicating with boys. Even after working with boys for several years, counseling them, evaluating them for ADHD and learning challenges, and advising schools on how best to educate them, it was not until I attempted to work with boys in groups that I fully grasped the best way to connect with their psychology. This includes the best way to communicate with and know boys.

Let me describe what happened to me. Several schools near where I was practicing psychology became aware of my work with school-age boys, and asked me to start a social skills group for kids between the ages of 9 and 12. Most of these boys had some type of learning disability or ADHD, and all struggled with some degree of social awkwardness. It seemed like a natural fit for my professional interests, and I'd been working with socially challenged men for several years.

Parents were enthusiastic, and the group quickly enrolled. Unfortunately, it became apparent that the boys were not nearly as enthusiastic as their parents. Greeting the young members of my group in the waiting room, they sat with arms folded, grim expressions, and little eye contact. As I escorted the group of boys to my office I could sense them trudging along with a combination of dread and boredom. That was pretty much the tone of the groups in those early days. The boys didn't want to be there, and soon I didn't want to be there either. Over a few weeks, I went from feeling confident and enthusiastic, to feeling frustrated and irritable. If you've ever felt the sting of kids who don't return your enthusiasm for something that's very important to you, then you know what I'm talking about.

My self-esteem was taking a hit from this experience. Up until that point, I'd thought that I was pretty good at working with boys. I believed that my commitment to improving their lives would be enough to win their confidence and trust. I was wrong. It got so frustrating that I thought about ending the group. My basic thoughts were, "Who needs this? Why am I putting myself through this?" Failure has a way of playing tricks on your mind, and it wasn't long before I'd backed myself into a corner of negative reasoning. "If they hate coming this much, then maybe boys aren't supposed to be in groups like mine." Yet even as I had those thoughts, I was affected by nagging questions like, "What am I doing wrong?" and "Why aren't these kids responding to me?" Those questions spurred me to think harder and more flexibly about what I could do differently.

To be honest, for all my thinking, I couldn't find the right answer to my problem. And then I had an unexpected breakthrough. One weekend, I was watching television when the movie *Gladiator,* starring Russell Crowe, came on. I'd heard about but hadn't seen the film. That Friday night I was riveted, watching the story of Maximus unfold. In fact, I was so captivated I watched the movie again on Saturday and Sunday (it was on the TNT network, in the days when TNT showed the same movie Friday, Saturday, and Sunday nights). By the time I'd seen the movie for the third time, I realized that *Gladiator* provided an inspiration for connecting with the boys in my group! Right in the opening scene of the film, when Maximus is rallying his troops for battle, he recognizes the tension and gravity of the moment. He understands that his men need something from him — a sentiment or some type of credo to unite them as they face a terrifying, chaotic experience. And Maximus reminds them to have "strength and honor." It's a credo with massive resonance for males, and as portrayed in the film, the soldiers under Maximus' command become galvanized and more united when they hear it. "Strength and honor" spoke to their courage, integrity, and fortitude. This rallying call is a magical

Hollywood moment, and I knew it was exactly what I needed for my boy's group.

The next week, greeting the seven boys in my group, I began in a new manner. Extending a fist, I said, "Strength and honor Dylan. Strength and honor Richard. Strength and honor Jake." The phrase was delivered in a no-nonsense, enthusiastic style, with a clear, resonant vocal tone. I meant to indicate we were embarking on serious, important business together. I also taught each of the boys in my group to greet me the same way, to extend a vertical fist until their fist met mine, and to say, "Strength and honor, Dr. Cox" immediately after I greeted them. The greeting was different from a fist bump. I emphasized maintaining some rigidity in your arm, making direct eye contact, and the importance of speaking with sufficient volume and clarity. Following this greeting, I marched with the boys to my office, and we began to develop new ways to communicate with one another. "Strength and honor" paved the way for effort, respect, and expressions of empathy between us all.

Everything changed that day. The atmosphere of the group, and the boys' enthusiasm for our work reversed direction. The power of the experience is not only in the associations boys make with the words, it's also in the vocal tone used to deliver the greeting. Done in the right way, *"strength and honor" reinforces the way boys want to feel about themselves.* With that greeting, we transformed ourselves from a group concerned with individual deficits and inadequacies, to a band of brothers committed to serving one another. We were ready to slay dragons if necessary.

From this humble, simple, but effective starting point, I've been able to connect with boys in a way I wouldn't have thought possible. In the pages ahead, I'll explain in practical terms how you too can crack the boy code. I will show you exactly how to start and sustain great conversations with the boys you care most about. Everything you need to know about being closer and more connected to your son, students, or players can be found in *Cracking the Boy Code*. That is a bold assertion, but in the years since I first discovered the power of "strength and honor," I've used this psychological approach with boys around the world. I have greeted entire assemblies of boys, nearly a thousand strong, with this unique approach.

Words alone do not accomplish magic, but when we develop a strong and persistent spirit to match those words, we become more compelling, and effective for boys.

It's not my intention to oversimplify the challenges of communicating with young people. You need more than a simple phrase to have a great conversation, or to build a great relationship. It's been my good fortune to travel and speak widely about my work with boys, including visiting some of the world's finest schools. I've addressed parents, teachers, and boys throughout North America, and in England, Australia, New Zealand, Singapore, and South Africa. Throughout, I have continued to work with families of all kinds, and with boys experiencing every imaginable kind of social, emotional, and cognitive difficulty. *Cracking the Boy Code* highlights what I've learned; it offers practical, straightforward strategies which you can begin using immediately. On behalf of your own boys, and those everywhere, I thank you for your interest in communicating and relating well, and for the compassion this interest implies. Let's get started!

Part I

Strategies and Techniques for Talking

Chapter 1

What Is Good Communication?

W E NEED TO BEGIN WITH A BASIC PREMISE: *good communication is effective communication.* Communicating well means getting through to another person, having them hear you and appreciate the point or value of what you are saying. Communication can be *instrumental*, as when we ask a basic question "What do you want for dinner?" This sort of communication is heard fairly well by boys, and it's also their favorite type to use: "Pass the milk. Can I have 20 bucks? You gonna eat all them fries?" Generally, it's not hard for boys to communicate basic questions or statements. It's the other type of conversation — *social communication* — which poses a challenge for boys. This is a serious issue because most important communication is inherently social. We communicate because we want to connect with another person. For example, what do most of us do if we want to get to know another person better? What would you do if you wanted to build more trust into a relationship? What would you do if you wanted someone to better understand your thinking or emotions? Of course, you would talk to them! Communicating is what our instincts tell us to do when we want to be closer to someone, when we want a stronger relationship.

Just because adults want a stronger relationship, however, doesn't mean boys want the same. Mostly they are a little scared of getting too close to adults and would rather remain somewhat undercover. When they do communicate with adults, they typically do so with a specific purpose, and that approach goes right along with the "bottom line" psychology of boys. Often, teenage boys think to themselves, "I'll

1

communicate when I want something." You've probably noticed that boys can be more relaxed when they talk with friends, but their behaviors are totally different when talking with adults.

Should we fight this tendency in boys, or get comfortable working with it? Definitely, the latter. Overcoming the distance between any two people begins with mutual acceptance. The longer we spend trying to bend people to our will, insisting that they think and act differently, the longer we will be frustrated. Even the youngest of boys is capable of a fiercely strong will, and it doesn't take much for a boy to win a communication war. He just stops talking!

I'm an optimist, and I'm going to assume you are flexible and willing to experiment with a different approach. First, let's agree that there is a degree of planning required to effectively communicate with boys. Let's also assume that the measure of whether our approach is working is how the boys respond. Sometimes that means giving us a signal that we've been heard, like raising their eyes to meet ours. Sometimes it amounts to more, like changing a behavior, or taking the initiative to do something without having to be reminded multiple times. (If you've ever met a boy under age 18, you are no doubt familiar with this challenge.) When we do get a response, it tells us we are building a bridge between our minds and theirs. Think of how a bridge can be used by people to advance or retreat. The key point of communicating with boys is to give them a bridge, a way to connect with us when they need to. Sure, at times they may choose to withdraw, but a well-built bridge will invite boys across time and again. To build this bridge, we must know something about the minds of boys, and that is largely the focus of Part I of this book. We will especially need to understand how listening style, apprehension, social awkwardness, and sometimes adolescent self-absorption, can be roadblocks to that bridge. It has become popular to refer to these problems as pathologies (diagnosable conditions), but the problem with that perspective is that it makes all of boyhood a "disease." I believe this is a serious problem — for us more than them.

Our number one priority is to get through to boys so that our support and guidance can fully register. Yet being an effective communicator has another important benefit: we become role models for boys so that in time they can replicate our good communication strategies. Good teachers use empathy and strategy to create a connection with their students all the time.

> Whenever we are communicating well, we are also teaching.

Form and Content

I've already described two types of communication, instrumental and social, and emphasized that, in this book, we want to work on the social type. Communication also has two dimensions that are critical to remember: *form* and *content*. If we focus exclusively on the content of communication (what it is that we want to say), we lose awareness of the form of our communication. By form, I mean the way we say things (the tone, volume, and speed of our speech). I also mean how we use nonverbal signals like facial expressions and body language. Although most people focus intently on what they want to say, they pay much less attention to the way they speak. When we feel as though our words have been misunderstood, it's often the case that the tone of our speech, facial expressions, and body language told a different story than our words.

> **Major hint:** It is the *form* of communication that resonates deeply for boys, and which they remember for hours and days after a conversation. This is Rule #1, and I'll remind you of it often. Your tone is "louder" than your words. How you say things lingers longer than what you say.

Boys remember the way that you looked at them after reviewing a report card, and they remember the sound of your voice when you congratulated them after a sporting event, and how that way of speaking differed from the way you sounded after the school play. Most boys are sensitive to the tone of your voice, and the emotions conveyed by your face. By the way, it's not only an angry tone or look we need to think about. Boys are especially sensitive to signals that suggest they are not smart, or need to be treated like a "child." Even when you want to respond to their apparent immaturity, remember that you are building a relationship fueled by respect. More on this massively important topic later.

Taking them seriously is the single most important and significant privilege you grant a young person.

If I had a choice between giving you the skills to change the form of your communication or telling you exactly what to say, I would choose the former. (Fortunately, I'm going to have a chance to advise on both!) I think it would surprise many, but the truth is that boys listen better to people who take charge of the nonverbal signals in their communication. You have probably heard many times, in self-help books or on television, that nonverbal communication is as important as verbal communication. This is true, and in this book, I want to be very specific about what that means for communicating with boys. When we talk about vocal tone and nonverbal signaling, such as eye contact, I'll be emphasizing exactly how your voice and face "set the table" for great conversations.

Good communication also relies on emotional intelligence. Essentially, we must detect what other people are thinking or feeling and know how to respond to those thoughts and feelings. Everybody knows people who do this well, and there is usually at least one person in most families who has this type of intuition. An entire science of emotional intelligence (EQ) has emerged in research, and many books have been written on this topic. EQ begins with excellent self-awareness, and an understanding of how you come across to other people.1 As you work with the ideas in this book, I want you to become a student of your own communication. It's not enough to know that you effectively get through to people; I want you to become aware of what you're doing right, and when you're communicating well. It's that sort of awareness that takes you to the next level and inspires confidence and creativity. And, by the way, as you learn strategies for getting through to the important boys in your life, you'll notice that these skills are extremely helpful when it comes to communicating with others as well.

Remember that your voice and speech are extensions of what is in your mind. Each of us knows this intuitively, which is why we pay such close attention to the way other people talk when we want to understand what they are thinking or feeling. This is also why people can sometimes become offended by another person's words: tone gives words an "edge." Most of us take communication very personally. Words are more than abstractions; they come from the deepest places of belief and emotion. That's why we go over another person's phrasing again and again in our mind — especially when there has been a conflict of some sort. As most of us have learned, it's hard to retract your words once they've been spoken. Boys may act indifferent to what we say, but they are absorbing the feeling of words and tone, and they're using those signals to draw conclusions about us.

What type of communication works well for boys?
Communication that is easiest for boys to digest has three important qualities:

• *Vocabulary* that is familiar.
• *Phrasing* that is nonjudgmental.
• *Tone* that is matter-of-fact.

Talking and Momentum

A basic, but critical measure of good communication, is that it moves a relationship forward. That's also a basic condition of healthy relationships: they grow and evolve. This is especially true when one person in the relationship is still growing up, because that person is changing dynamically, almost daily. I'm not saying that every relationship must constantly improve. I think that's unrealistic. But I do think relationships must adjust to life and situational changes. Good communication is key. On a micro level, we can see this in a very straightforward way. For example, do your questions or statements bring out responses that eventually become a conversation? Does that conversation have enough relational "energy" to sustain itself? (Do you ever feel like saying, "Dude, this isn't like TV, you have to talk back. I'm feeling very lonely here."?) And does conversation include topics that are interesting to both of you? Please note the word *both*; good communication with boys should often touch upon topics that are interesting and relevant to both parties. I know from experience, however, that not all adults recognize or believe in this sort of mutuality. Some people think good parenting is lecturing from a point of authority: parents do the talking, and kids do the listening. Dads are famous for this approach, because they've been waiting for years for it to be their turn! My dad sometimes communicated with me in this way, and although I know he did so with good intentions, it was still annoying.

If we define good communication with boys as first and foremost that which gets their attention, we will have skipped the fundamental step of building a relationship. If you're a Type A personality — all business, and not a second to waste — you may try to resist this idea. You just want to cut to the chase, right? Sorry, but there is no practical way to demand the attention of boys just because we are older, have more status, or can speak really loud. (This might work at first, but then you'll have none of their attention when they turn 16 or 17 and can speak as loudly as you.) As a family therapist, trust me on this. Being authoritative is good; being authoritarian is bad. The difference between being a coach or a boss can determine whether a relationship has a future.

Building a relationship is not a matter of being clever, or putting someone in a hypnotic trance that forces them to listen. It's more about being authentic and respectful. We use respect and tone to encourage boys to listen and respond. This is the secret of "strength and honor." When we are communicating well, the other person feels as though they have been included in our *mental orbit*. When I refer to this orbit, I'm talking about the psychological space of primary concern — the place where most of our focus is. Great communication is a joining of two or more orbits, with each person in a conversation feeling invested and heard. For example, if you're one of millions of parents concerned your son is spending so much time on social media that his homework is neglected, I strongly advise spending some time connecting around his interest in social media before you lay down the gauntlet and threaten to take his phone.

Think of a boy's interests and focus as his *mental orbit*. Then think about what you need to do to be a part of that orbit. I guarantee that your nonverbal signals, and talking about relevant topics, will accelerate the process. Practice, practice, practice.

To connect with another person's orbit, we must understand their priorities. More specifically, we should register what is important to that person, and what they might like to talk to us about. Right now, chances are your son is not sophisticated enough to be as concerned about your priorities and interests as you are in his. But he does want your love and approval. As the adult in the relationship, you may have to enlarge your "orbit" while he's learning to relate to others with more skill. So often, good communication with boys begins with a topic that is of special interest to them. It's certainly better to capture a person's interest, rather than trying to command his attention by startling him or somehow making him anxious that there will be consequences if he doesn't listen. It would be great if kids could translate our upset feelings as a sign of compassion and loving concern. But they don't. They mostly feel adult upset as criticism and reprimand. Once they hear that angry tone, they can barely pay attention to the words.

Sometimes, boys can assume the look of someone who is listening without turning their full attention to us. When they do, it is usually because they are afraid they are going to get flak. Unfortunately, kids who adopt this attitude are often so anxious that their capacity to listen effectively, and remember what has been said, is diminished.

I recognize that parents and other adults want to communicate with boys in a variety of ways, not all of which are directive. Many parents would like to know their sons at a deeper level, and wish that their sons would open up and talk to them. Two decades of work with families has taught me this is an important need for parents, because without an opportunity to converse about important things with kids, we feel as though we are being excluded — and it hurts. Countless mothers, especially, long for closeness they had with younger boys, which has all but disappeared by the time boys become tweens.

Conversely, if you have a child who tends to be somewhat obsessive, you may feel as though you're included in too many judgments. Most adults, however, would like to be included or consulted regarding important decisions. I don't necessarily mean matters of greatest privacy. Anyone who has been a child understands that sometimes there are things you don't want to discuss until you are ready. Concerning more routine decisions and thoughts that make up our days, adult guidance can be consistently useful. If you follow the guidance in this book, you'll learn how to provide that guidance without slipping into lecturing or scolding. You will absolutely feel more optimistic about getting through to boys in a way that works for them. You'll have a communication style that makes boys happy to have you in their corner.

Communication and Gender

Is communication harder for boys than girls? It depends on what you mean by "harder." In some situations, boys can talk freely. For example, most boys are more verbal in public than private settings. Think of a time when boys are hanging out with their male peers. In those situations, I think we see lots of bold communication, with boys using their words to vie for attention and status. In my own research, boys have told me that their ability to persuade peers is an important sign of status. It means others are giving you respect. But let's be clear, that sort of public talk usually lacks authenticity. It's closer to grandstanding or a sales pitch than it is to sincere expression. I accept this because I think *that sort of communication is a developmental need for boys.* If we make them feel self-conscious to talk that way in our presence, they'll learn to be more secretive. Boys are not about to restrain bravado because for many there is too much at stake — especially their standing among peers.

Other types of communication are a greater challenge for boys. I'll get into these issues in more depth in the next two chapters, and we'll see that the short-term memory challenges of boys, the volume of sound they hear, and their tendency to go on thought tangents can make personal or private communication challenging. There is no single consensus about the cause of these challenges for many males, but some of the difficulties appear to be based in the brain. For example, did you know that estrogen is more helpful to working memory than testosterone?[2] This means boys lack a hormone that has been shown to be particularly helpful in remembering the chunks of information that allow us to recount important experiences, or remember things like how to study for a test. Research has also shown that boys have a higher proportion of white matter to gray matter in the cortex of the brain.[3] And it's the gray matter that is responsible for making short-range connections within the brain. The prefrontal cortex — the place where attention comes from — seems to be somewhat more efficient in girls than boys, although differences tend to diminish over time.

These issues are not trivial. They have much to do with the differences we perceive between genders. I believe that these differences also stem from the different ways boys and girls are socialized, but there's no getting around biological differences. As of this writing, biological brain difference is unfortunately still a contested issue, which only distracts us from what we can do to constructively improve communication with boys. Some believe that asserting biological brain difference is a gateway to suggesting a hierarchy, or might result in the unfair allocation of school resources. I am opposed to both of those possibilities. My sole purpose in identifying the apparent processing differences of boys is to strategize about better communication with them.

You Must Practice

We could probably agree that some skills come easier to some people than others. But most skills are acquired through constructive practice. All the skills in this book will become more available if you can commit to practicing them on a consistent basis. I know most of us don't think of communication as something we need to practice. Maybe it isn't, if we are only thinking about how easy it is to talk with friends or other family members. Boys are a different story. You are communicating across generations. If you are female, you are also communicating across gender. *The simple fact is that the better you can hear your own voice, and how it registers with boys, the more effective you'll be in getting through to boys.* A major mistake is assuming that when we ask logical and rational questions, we have essentially done our job. Sorry, but that is not the case when it comes to relating to boys. Our questions may be logical, but if we don't pose them in a way that invites participation, we haven't moved a conversation and a relationship forward.

The reason communication warrants our careful attention is that it is at the center of how we present ourselves and the impressions we leave with other people. How effectively we communicate sets up the possibility for future communication. One of the best feelings you can have after talking with boys is the sense that both of you are looking forward to the next chance to talk. If you struggle in communicating with your son or students, you've probably felt the sting of the opposite: there's nothing to say, and the conversation stalls. This happens to all adults, at least occasionally. I've spent years cultivating my own communication skills with boys, and it still happens to me from time to time. Sometimes it's hard to find the thread of common interest that brings two people together. You may wonder, "Why is it so hard when we both belong to the same family?" You'll do a whole lot better if you open your ears and listen closely to the things that boys say when there is no self-consciousness. There's almost always a hint in those moments for attentive listeners. Make a mental note to start your next conversation with that theme.

When all else fails, you can rely on a precious human commodity — truthfulness. When we are truthful, we are also authentic, and often a little vulnerable. Boys sense this about us, and recognize when we have dropped our defenses. In response, they feel more comfortable dropping their own. Boys respond well to people that *walk the walk*, as well as those who *talk the talk*. For example, they like it when they see adults taking the kinds of emotional risks that adults are encouraging them to take. This is important for fathers or male mentors to do, because our society often tells boys that showing vulnerability, like being unsure of yourself, is not masculine. Often, traits associated with femininity are both overtly and covertly devalued. This is contrary to the "strength and honor" perspective, which emphasizes personal integrity, respect, and a willingness to learn what you don't yet understand. Good communication always involves a kind of transaction. Your openness is exchanged for boys' attention and participation. The attitude and style I'm recommending here might sound a little like skills the leader of group therapy uses, and they are. If you are leading a conversation, you are the facilitator, and it's up to you to model emotional skills and honesty.

> What is the hidden, and most important ingredient, in good communication with boys?
> RESPECT

Respect and Seriousness

OK, let me challenge a widely held assumption about how to get along with boys. It's the belief that great relationships with boys are built on lots of jokes, bending rules, and horsing around as much as possible. Hey, I know boys like these things, but they are not the qualities that win the day for adults who want a sustainable, respectful relationship with boys. Don't get me wrong, I believe humor is valuable, but not as valuable as respect and seriousness. Does this surprise you? I think it would surprise many people, and I'm not sure that everybody will — at least initially — agree with me. If you're thinking, like many parents, that the most important thing that your son needs from you is love, then I've got some bad news for you. Most boys already assume they've got that in the bag. What I mean is that boys are not sitting at home anxiously wondering if their parents love them. I understand that in a few sad cases, boys may in fact need to be assured that they are loved. But I also know that readers of a book like this one have already met that need.

For most boys, the most important way to demonstrate your love is through respect. When treated with respect, a boy senses that he is being taken seriously. That seriousness confirms his positive status. When you project seriousness, you are making your own mental orbit visible and accessible. This transparency is a natural and strong attractor for boys and young men. You will find respect and seriousness throughout this book because they are the most important, yet most under-discussed themes in the psychology of boyhood. Hours of school assemblies and parental lectures attempt to convey morals to boys. Though well intended, they usually neglect the most effective form of appeal — respect. When I am fortunate enough to have a chance to demonstrate the power of respect at school gatherings, it is an eye-opener for everybody.

"We Could Be Heroes": Connecting with Boys' Ideal Selves

Ultimately, good communication helps to connect boys with their "ideal selves." This is the sense of self that they fantasize about being — the person that they imagine themselves to be in a perfect world. It is of great importance for boys to connect with this ideal self, to feel like they have a chance to incorporate idealism in their day-to-day lives. This possibility is what the magic of Harry Potter books is about, and it's also why many boys admire athletic heroism. What we need to remember is that boys are also looking for an appreciation of their ideals in their communication with adults. Adults' respect and seriousness help to convey openness to boys' ideals, as do questions that give boys a chance to experiment with those ideals. There is in most boys a yearning to be something more than they are. This may sound childish or entitled, but it is the nature of boyhood and, in my view, the nature of manhood for many. I believe we must hold awareness of striving for ideals in mind as we converse with boys. I've noticed that understanding boys' yearnings is as important when talking about the need to rake leaves or care for the dog, as it is when talking about prospective vocations.

In this chapter, I've oriented you to some basic principles of good communication, suggesting that the ultimate goal is building great relationships. I've also emphasized some of the unique aspects of boys' psychology, and how they play a role in boys' expectations of us. We're going to look at these issues in greater depth, with lots more detail about practical skills. For now, here's what is important:

Remember:
• Social communication is the greatest communication challenge for boys.

- Vocabulary, phrasing, and tone set the stage for great conversations.
- Get inside a boy's mental orbit by paying attention to what is important to him.
- Be generous with your respect.

Points to Consider:

- When I communicate, how do I sound to boys?
- Do I notice my nonverbal signals (volume, pace, pitch, gestures, facial expression) when speaking?
- What is my priority in communicating with my son or student?

Chapter 2

Is He Hearing You?

T WO BASIC THINGS WE NEED TO CONSIDER are that boys don't always hear enough of what we say, and what they do hear is often at least partially inaccurate. Many attempts at talking to boys can be thwarted by the boys' selective hearing, poor listening skills, and distraction. Let's take a closer look at these challenges to better understand what's going on when we are trying to communicate. Then, we'll strategize about how to get around these obstacles.

The brain differences of boys are a hot topic in the fields of psychology and neuroscience. I've written about these differences in my other books, and have spent the past decade talking to schools and parents about the effects of these differences. The point of this book is to examine how the psychology of boys affects their communication and our ability to get through to them. It's hard to quantify the extent of gender difference in communication and social behaviors; is it an average 20% difference or 5% difference? I'm not sure any scientist would be prepared to come to such broad conclusions. The range of difference varies according to what kinds of cognitive abilities we might examine. Those who minimize the importance of differences point out that *within group differences* (among boys and girls) are greater than the difference between boys and girls. This is true. Like most scientists, I believe that the genders are much more alike than they are different. But this doesn't invalidate the fact that there are differences, and that they do matter.[4] It's human nature to pay close attention to differences, perhaps for the very reason that we are so much more alike than different. If everyone on your street has a silver car, the small elements of a car's trim become increasingly important to recognizability. The more similar the general characteristic of things are, the more attention we give to whatever small differences might exist. Simply put, differences interest us.

Functionally speaking, it's small differences that change the way we act or perform a task. So, it's no surprise that boys' hearing is often perceived as being less effective than girls. By that I mean that boys don't seem to hear information as well as girls, and tend to be more forgetful of what they do hear.[5] One factor may be hormones. For example, it appears that estrogen, a female hormone, is significantly more helpful in working memory ability than testosterone. This helps to explain why girls typically learn to read earlier and more efficiently than boys. When women experience a reduction in estrogen during menopause, they too have problems with working memory.[6]

Stimulation Rules

Although there are some biologically based reasons for hearing differences,[7] the most important differences for us to focus on here are related to the *psychology* of boys, and how that psychology affects listening and comprehension. One particularly relevant psychological attribute for many males is a high degree of self-absorption. This assertion may be perceived as criticism, but I've been working with boys for long enough that I've long since let go of being irritated about the situation. If you've spent much time with boys, you may have experienced how difficult it can be to break into their mental orbit. Have you ever tried talking to your son at a time when he's engaged in an activity that's highly stimulating, and totally absorbing to him? If so, you've seen how things that are personally relevant and exciting to boys can cause them to lose a sense of balance and priority. Boys who might normally be polite and responsive can forget something as basic as making polite eye contact.

Sometimes when boys get deeply entangled in personal concerns, we tend to moralize about their behavior, as though self-absorption were a character problem. We say things like, "he could respond if he wanted to," or, "he's not trying hard enough." And we may think to ourselves that a lack of eye contact and responsiveness is an active decision on his part — that he's using a lack of eye contact to "say" that we are unimportant. I think this is a big mistake. It leads us down a path toward hurt feelings and, eventually, anger. Neither parents nor kids benefit from this way of thinking. It's better and more accurate at such moments to realize that stimulation rules the psychology of boys, and if we want their undivided attention we should find a way to break through — to be stimulating.

As a rule, more stimulation is better. Providing stimulation (through volume, pitch, eye contact, and animated communication) will help you to align your attention with a boy's. In many cases, more stimulation can simply mean more volume. I don't mean to sound simplistic here, but we should recognize that there are practical benefits to speaking more loudly. I've learned this from thousands of hours working with boys, of all levels of ability, and with a wide variety of personalities. Of course, speaking more loudly doesn't necessarily mean that we are speaking angrily. Please spend some time reflecting on this idea: *Speaking louder doesn't mean being angry.* In fact, the challenge is learning how to speak in a way that conveys interest and engagement, more than it does irritation. *Our own emotions can become "magnets" for boys.* When we feel excited or enthusiastic, it naturally draws the attention of others. Boys will be drawn to our enthusiasm, and will want to be co-participants in whatever news or idea we are excited about. For sure, there must be a degree of authenticity to this approach. If we're only faking excitement to get boys' attention, they'll see through us every time, and they will withhold participation.

> Our own positive emotions can become "magnets" for boys, causing them to want to be around us, and to understand what we're feeling good about.

Left Hemisphere Thinkers in a Right Hemisphere World

If you observe boys casually interacting in a social situation, maybe in conversation, or working together in a classroom, you'll probably notice they have distinct nonverbal communication tendencies. They often look forward with a kind of blank stare. It's not that they aren't thinking, because they are thinking about a lot. Still, it can be difficult to guess what many boys are thinking or feeling. Maybe you've noticed how little their facial expressions change, even as interesting and provocative content is presented. Why is this? Is it a deliberate attempt to hide emotion? No, but it is a significant issue with respect to how boys are processing different kinds of social information in their brains.

We shouldn't oversimplify the functions of different regions of the brain like the left and right hemisphere. As noted by John Medina in *Brain Rules*, we can safely trust some established conclusions from neuroscience about the basic roles of the hemispheres. For example, human beings tend to make sense of social situations, and visual cues like facial expressions, with the *right* hemisphere of their brain. Conversely, they tend to process language and logic in the *left* hemisphere of the brain. I want to be careful not to digress into a detailed examination of brain hemisphere differences; these differences are complex and beyond the scope of this book. Like many psychologists and scientists, I cannot fully isolate functions within one hemisphere of the brain. But I do think it's fair to say that, with respect to the communication challenges of boys, many boys are left hemisphere thinkers in a right hemisphere world.

> It seems to be our right hemisphere that is critical in helping us to sort out the full meaning of what people say to us.

Let me give you an example: if someone says to you "my dog died last week" *your brain's left hemisphere tends to hear just the facts:* You had a dog / The dog died / It happened last week. Imagine a computer speaking these lines without any emotion, and you get the general feeling of how the left hemisphere "hears" content — even very emotional content.

It's up to your brain's right hemisphere to use contextual information so you have a more complete understanding of what was said. So instead of just hearing "my dog died last week," your right hemisphere notices the facial expression, body language, and vocal nuances of the person who made the statement. For example, you could notice how a person's eyes conveyed their feelings, and that this helped you to understand how to respond to their statement in an appropriate, helpful way. Are they very sad? Are they over it already? Is he or she looking for consolation and support, or do they want to be left alone? All the nonverbal cues that can help you to answer these questions are processed by the brain's right hemisphere.

Unfortunately, many boys have right hemispheres that have partially gone to sleep. In part because of not noticing important information, and because of that nagging problem with working memory that I mentioned earlier. Consequently, they struggle to comprehend complete messages. When the right hemisphere is asleep, only the factual part of a message or idea is taken in. And when boys only get part of the message, they're often confused about how to react. Whenever I'm studying boys in social situations, I must remember that their faces don't always tell me the full extent of what they're thinking or feeling. Even those boys who do perceive nonverbal cues with their right hemisphere may not be translating that understanding into a facial expression we can interpret.

Because I've spent quite a few years working with boys who have autism spectrum disorders, I have become particularly sensitive to communication challenges. Sometimes when I'm trying to get through to boys who are affected by higher functioning autism, they often stare back blankly, or with a somewhat quizzical look. There may be very little movement in their eyes, or sometimes they avert their eyes, making almost no eye contact. Usually, these boys' voices have a monotone quality, concealing any hint of emotion. If, in those circumstances, I assume that boys are not listening to me, or don't understand what I'm saying, I will often be mistaken — and worse, less helpful to them than I can be. That's why we should have frequent check-ins with boys as we are talking to them. We want to know if they are hearing us accurately. You also want to be able to gauge boys' interest in what you are saying.

Without the benefit of social perceptual skills, boys are missing whole frequencies of information that affect their social capability. Check in often to make sure you are being heard accurately.

Detecting Nonverbal Communication Differences

The practical implications of limited social awareness are everywhere. Here's an example encountered frequently. A boy is referred to see me by his school because he tends to be reactive, and is sometimes physically impulsive in such a way that it surprises his teachers and classmates. For example, he's too rough with other students, roams around the classroom at inappropriate times, climbs the furniture, or messes with another student's property. The school would like this student to get his emotions and impulses under better control. I agree to take the case, and then do an initial consultation with the boy and his family. During the evaluation, this boy acts normally and says conventional things. I ask questions that probe his understanding of right and wrong, and he passes with flying colors. Basically, he seems like a normal, capable boy.

Over the course of years, however, I've developed some strategies for examining factors that affect boys' behavior, especially impulsivity. I begin by asking some basic questions that involve a boy's ability to understand emotional circumstances and idioms. For example, I might ask him to explain the meaning of emotive sentences like: "She cried and cried at her son's wedding." "Why does someone cry at a wedding?" Or I might ask, "What does this sentence mean: She knew if she didn't tell someone she would explode?" Or maybe, "What does it mean that a leopard can't change his spots?"

I want to find out whether the boy understands that tears can be an expression of joy, and that "exploding" is a metaphor for becoming emotionally upset. This undoubtedly sounds obvious to you — but there are many, many eight-to-ten-year-olds who struggle with understanding these "frequencies" of communication. Clinically speaking, these kids are understood to have limited pragmatic communication skills. They miss important communication cues, and they tend to misinterpret the verbal and nonverbal communication of others — including yours! Very often, they tend to be literal thinkers.

In general, literal thinking is an enormous problem among males of all ages. Literal thinking can lead to misinterpretation, and unwarranted, out of proportion, reactions. And words are not the only challenge. There is also lots of misinterpretation of physical cues. For example,

Ben pushes Dylan who then bumps into Andrew. Suddenly, Andrew turns around and swings at Dylan for bumping into him. In this situation Andrew does not consider the possibility that Dylan himself was pushed, and is not to blame for bumping into Andrew. Further, he doesn't understand that what he experienced was the result of some relatively friendly horsing around between Dylan and Ben, who intended absolutely no harm to Andrew. But Andrew's brain appears not prepared to deduce the meaning of this sequence of actions, and he quickly assigns a flawed interpretation to what has happened to him.

Imagine that a boy like Andrew experiences this type of situation repeatedly, each time misinterpreting cause and effect. Not only will his teachers, school principal, and possibly his parents become very frustrated, but Andrew himself will become annoyed and possibly depressed that he's constantly blamed, feeling always like he is the victim. Is this scenario familiar to you? If you've spent any time around groups of boys, chances are at least one of them has had this type of thinking and reaction.

Before we go any further, let's clarify that *underreacting is as common as overreacting.* Some boys don't feel like they have enough friends, especially in school. Usually, such boys need to learn a more open and receptive communication style. Lots of boys need to learn how to send positive signals to other kids. The difficulty here is that if you are never more reactive than a rock, other people can't gauge what you are thinking, and whether you are at all interested in them. The stone faces of some boys can be off-putting. Until you get to know them, many boys won't reveal if they find you to be helpful, likable, or even interesting. In those situations, remind yourself that there's much more to this person than meets the eye, and it can be revealed over time.

Can He Say What He Means? Does He Know What He Feels?

Boys are as emotionally complex as everyone else. The problem is that much of that complexity never seems to make it to the surface — to their faces and voices — where we could detect and respond. Instead, boys' emotions stay locked away in a place where neither they nor we can benefit. A useful way to think about this situation is that there is a conduit between their emotions, and their faces and voices, which is blocked. The blockage could be fear, anxiety, lack of confidence, social deficits or something else. Whatever the cause, the question becomes how to unblock the conduit, allowing the full complexity of a person to surface. In psychology, we call this sort of blockage *alexithymia*, which translates from Greek as *without words for emotion*. A better term is *dyslexithymia*, which means *problems with words for emotion*. I can't say I've ever met a boy who has absolutely no words for emotion, but I've met many who could use a few more.

This is a problem that affects people of all ages, and it does so for similar reasons. The conduit between emotions and their expression is a two-way street. Not only are emotions potentially blocked from being expressed, their lack of practice *expressing emotions* can hinder healthy self-awareness. How does this work? Well, people's intelligence and capability needs *situational practice* to fully develop. Even a person born with incredible potential needs opportunities to practice his gifts for them to be activated and mature. It can be difficult to build self-awareness without some practice in expressing what you feel and know about yourself. Why is this important? Because you can't adequately develop empathy for other people until you have a basic understanding of your own emotions. Empathy begins with self-awareness. You need some basic awareness of your own emotional experiences to effectively relate to others.

Silence Creates Tension

If you've ever gotten stuck while conversing with a quiet boy at home or in school, you are probably familiar with how long and awkward silences can slow or block conversation. Silence has a way of undoing the flow of conversation. It tends to increase anxiety and self-consciousness, and establishes an awkward precedent for the rhythm of conversation. One of the simplest approaches is to avoid open-ended questions, at least at the beginning of a conversation. You may have been taught that to be a good conversationalist, it's wise to ask open-ended questions. Questions like "what do you like about your school?" spark less momentum than simple, forced-choice questions, requiring a "yes" or "no" answer: "Do you like school?" "Is the food in your cafeteria good?" "Will you be going to the concert?"

Usually, when interviewing boys for the first time in my clinical office, I tend to ask questions very rapidly. Sometimes, I barely give boys enough time to answer before asking the next question. This approach surprises many parents, who are sitting next to the child being interviewed. This might seem counterintuitive to you as well. It would have seemed unusual to me many years ago when I began treating boys, but now it feels entirely natural, and I believe that boys generally enjoy this approach. This is because it seems friendly, energetic, and interested. Sometimes the questions are so easy that the exchanges become speedy. This develops rapport and confidence in communicating. For a boy between six and nine, I might ask "Is your teacher tall? Taller than you? Is she funny? Is she better at teaching reading or math? Do you have math before or after lunch? Who do you sit with at lunch? Do you have enough time to eat lunch? Do you ever eat with your fingers?" I might ask all these questions in about a minute. I state them with little or no emotion, which relaxes boys, and jumpstarts our relationship. The answers are not important. It's the relationship and rapport I want to build. The best thing that can happen after an initial meeting is for a boy to say or think to himself, "that guy is easy to talk to."

For a boy between 11 and 14, I'm more likely to ask questions about extracurricular activities like sports, clubs, or any type of game interest. But I use the same cadence, and the same strategy as a means of getting things going. With older adolescent boys, I slow things down a bit. Typically, I try to match my communication style to theirs. If they sit in a slouched manner, I do the same. If they make little eye contact, I do as well. This may change as the relationship develops, but initially it's a primary way of establishing rapport and comfort. When I mirror other's nonverbal cues, I demonstrate that I am paying attention to the boy's state of mind, which is a form of empathic communication, even if it seems counterintuitive.

Meeting boys where they are at, particularly in your first conversations, builds trust and confidence. You can't build a relationship with someone if they are put off by your manner, or find it unlikable.

Electronic Interference

As if communicating with boys weren't difficult enough, we are now challenged to communicate with boys whose minds have been shaped by a steady stream of electronica: games, video, television, internet, and other forms of electronic media. There are serious short- and long-term effects of this electronic invasion. Some studies find that games can quicken some cognitive processes,[8] while others have noted that young people have more problems with sustained attention.[9] Basically, young people can't pay attention for very long, especially if the primary focal point is low stimulation, like someone talking about a topic that is of minimal personal interest. Without a doubt, one of the greatest challenges that teachers face is a generation of kids who aren't particularly good at listening. This phenomenon has changed the tempo and atmosphere of school, and we can be certain that reaching minds that have been overstimulated by electronics will continue to be a challenge.

In addition, continuous electronics make kids irritable. You can't play a video game for four hours and not be affected by some degree of grouchiness. I know that kids might be thrilled to begin a game session, but eventually the endless animations, sounds, and graphics are debilitating. The brain gets so supercharged with the onslaught of visual and auditory stimulation that it has trouble de-escalating when the game turns off. This also has the effect of creating a high degree of impatience, especially among younger boys. It's like the brain has been accustomed to nonstop stimulation; when the stimulation stops, the brain continues to demand more, and expresses its unhappiness with irritability and impatience.

There are also those boys who become so infatuated with games and other media that they decide it's the only type of activity they need in their life. They gradually withdraw from face-to-face interaction; they become content with relative isolation as long as they can talk to their friends online or through game playing. Are you stunned by all the rationalizations our society generates for allowing kids to have unlimited access to electronics? Collectively, we love technology, but I'm skeptical of claims that games teach social skills. In my view, these claims are rationalizations meant to make us feel better about an insane and growing addiction to electronics.

The bottom line is that kids are allowed access to electronics because they are everywhere, and because many adults don't have enough time to do things with kids that would take the place of electronics. Games may be fun and sometimes informative, but the degree to which young people play these games, to the exclusion of social interaction, is a lopsided way to approach the transition to adulthood. Yet I meet many boys and young men between 15 and 20, for whom games are their primary recreation. It's not surprising that their social communication skills are usually lacking, or at least awkward.

Boredom and Civility

Electronics have pushed boredom to the brink of extinction. We're raising a generation of kids who have lost the ability to be bored, and there are consequences to this trend.

I realize we are worried about young people losing momentum and productivity because of electronics. In my view, there is an even more significant problem with electronics, and it has to do with how we get along with each other. Boredom itself is not necessarily something we value or praise, but the capacity to tolerate boredom signifies a mind able to slow itself down long enough to reflect, and consider options.[10] A civil society relies on citizens' ability to reflect and consider. Civility implies the capacity for empathy, which is a whole lot more complex than manners. Everyone can learn manners, which are basically matters of habit. Boys learn to say thank you, hold a door open, and how to greet someone. These are good and important manners, but are a long way from being empathic.

To be truly civil means that you must be more considered — able to see the world through the eyes of another person. Civility requires a willingness to slow your mind down long enough to think about what people are feeling, or what they just said. Electronics threaten this capability because they nudge young minds toward speed and impatience. These effects aren't counterbalanced by positive messages embedded within a few games. Adults in general ignore the problem because it's hard to challenge lucrative industries, regardless of how the products affect young people.

Learning Styles

We've already seen that hearing can sometimes be a challenge for boys, and can be responsible for their difficulty in acquiring social knowledge. These same boys often struggle with sustaining good, reciprocal communication. Of course, there are some boys who gravitate toward learning through their ears, and there are those who learn best by watching, and by doing. There are currently many ways of understanding a person's learning style, and a quick internet search will yield at least a dozen different methods for assessing learning styles. I want to introduce you to a simple but quite useful way of thinking about learning differences. It focuses on three dominant *processing* or *learning styles*: visual, auditory, and kinesthetic. A person typically uses more than one sensory system to learn, but the idea is that one of three major systems tends to be the most dominant for an individual person. Boys who are *auditory processors* tend to have the least difficulty in school, because so much of school is made up of auditory-based information. As teachers are talking, these boys are listening, reasoning, and remembering. These boys are lucky enough to be able to use hearing as a means of acquiring the critical bits of information that lead to knowledge, and then produce good results on tests and other kinds of assignments. These same boys with good listening skills can do well in conversation at home, because they are in fact good listeners.

Visual processors rely upon their eyes as a primary means of gathering information and understanding. Boys who process visually want information to be presented in a visual way. They benefit greatly from watching a procedure they are trying to learn. For them, the more visual detail, the better. Good visuals give these boys a better chance of consolidating newly learned information into their long-term memories. Generally, there are more visually oriented boys than there are listening oriented boys.

Kinesthetic boys have the greatest difficulty in school. These kids like to move, often continuously, and they use movement as a way of mapping space in their minds. If you think about it, there's not too much of most school days that accommodates this type of activity and learning style. Kinesthetic boys would generally do better if they stood up throughout the school day, or at least had a chance to move around on a frequent basis. Kinesthetic boys also benefit from a sense of touch. Physical contact with others and things is a primary way these kids understand relationships and circumstances. On the other hand, if a student were going to be selected to organize a part of a classroom, a visually oriented boy would probably do best, and if a student were to be selected to read a passage from a book, in character, an auditory learner would likely excel.

When we want to communicate with a person, it's helpful to know something about his learning style. We can then embed this understanding in our communication with him.

A quick and useful way to detect a person's primary processing style is to notice where they look when drawing information from memory. For example, kinesthetic processors — those people who learn by doing, moving, and mapping space in their mind — usually look down when asked to recall a personal experience. These are the boys that tend to gravitate towards sports and other kinds of intense physical activities. You'll notice that these boys usually look in a downward direction. This reflects their strong physical connection with the ground; that's where their physical and emotional confidence originates — it is their zone of safety and stability. Make no mistake, these processing preferences have a way of sticking with us for life. For example, take a close look at how professional athletes sit when they are interviewed on television. You'll see that they keep their legs uncrossed, with their feet flat on the floor. They also tend to sit back and deeply in their seat, allowing a maximum of the receptors in their skin to contact the seat — this activates body awareness, and a sense of security. Usually their knees are spread, and they keep their body squared off with the interviewer. That sort of directness comes naturally to physical people. And it's not just males. If you watch female Olympians being interviewed, they do much the same.

When you see boys sit like this, they are going to have more difficulty connecting if you appeal only to their auditory processing channels. So, rather than saying something like "do you hear what I'm saying?" as you might for an auditory learner, or, "do you see what I'm saying?" as you would for a visual learner, you could say "do you get the feel of this?" The sensory word in each question connects with each boy's learning style, and in effect wakes up his mind-body learning system. For kinesthetic boys, I also look for a way to make friendly physical contact, such as a pat on the shoulder or back, or even a simple handshake. I might initiate a friendly game of catch as we speak. This is a way of reinforcing my connection to the boy, and it goes a long way toward helping him to relax and hear me.

Tuning into a boy's learning style is very much part of cracking the boy code. It works especially well for kinesthetic boys, but it resonates strongly for others as well. There's a firmness and directness in this awareness about connection which appeals to something primal in boys. I don't mean primal as in crude, rough, or violent. I do mean the primal desire boys have for friendly affiliation, cooperation, and a sense of capability. Those ideals are essential foundations for effective communication with boys.

You may be thinking "this a fine approach for certain types of kids, but I have a different type of son." Maybe he's someone who likes to study, is intensely interested in music, or tends to shy away from anything that is too athletic or physical. I would suggest that this same approach tends to be effective with a wide variety of boys and young men, although some will be more receptive at an earlier age. A fundamental premise of good communication with boys is respect and affiliation. It's impossible to overstate the importance of these processing signals. Please don't forget Rule #1 — it is always more important to set the stage with nonverbal signals than it is to explain yourself.

Remember
- Boys' hearing is less effective than girls.
- Boys' self-absorption undermines their working memory, and can be mistaken for rudeness or poor effort.
- The most important communication is nonverbal.

Points to Consider

- Is he missing, or misinterpreting, nonverbal signals?
- Is he a "literal thinker" — i.e. just getting the facts, without the emotional nuance of information?
- What is his primary learning pathway (auditory, visually, kinesthetic)?
- How can you mirror his nonverbal communication to increase his comfort?
- Have you tried a sequence of rapid, easy questions to break the ice?

Chapter 3

What's He Thinking?

M OST OF US ARE INTERESTED IN TALKING TO BOYS. The problem is that when we try, they are often nonresponsive, or at least under-responsive. Sometimes it's a battle just to get some eye contact. But why? What is all the resistance about? What are boys thinking when they stare back blankly, or avert eye contact altogether? Being guarded comes naturally to many, but that doesn't mean we can't understand boys' resistance, and then use insight to create closeness and trust.

In this chapter I will identify the *four major streams of thought that block boys from communicating with us.* You may assume that these are distortions on the part of boys, but I encourage you to be honest with yourself as we work through them. You may not intend to pry or lever-age information from your son, but he may feel that you are prying. The obstacles that hinder boys' communication come from the heart. They emanate from their deepest sources of anxiety, defensiveness, and irritation. Let's acknowledge that as far as boys are concerned, there are limits to a parent's "right" to know. If we expect to get through to boys, we must recognize the defenses they employ, and why.

#1 — You're Invading My Privacy

Perhaps the most common defensive thought for boys being pressed to communicate is "you're invading my personal space." They are even more likely to think along these lines when we try to communicate with them at inopportune times — when they are irritated, or caught up in something fun, stimulating, and unrelated to the topic of our query.

You should know that *boys have this thought without guilt or remorse.* Their premise is that "my thoughts belong to me, and I'm not obligated to share them with you." This is true. Evidence of this conviction is present early in the lives of boys. Many will make their first sign, "Keep Out," before they are eight years old.

The defensiveness of boys presupposes that we want to know their thoughts for some nefarious reason, like telling them they're wrong about something, or making them look foolish. Although our intentions are typically more positive, boys often persist in protecting their privacy. At some point this standoff becomes more about the significance of privacy than it does about any specific private matter. Tensions over privacy define many parent-child conversations; a simple attempt to talk about one small matter can turn into a power struggle about all sorts of things. How does this happen? Well, often our pursuit of answers to a question becomes unnecessarily intense and emotionally overwhelming. For example, you read a negative comment from a teacher about your son not turning in homework and want to immediately know, "why aren't you turning in your homework?" The answer is likely ordinary, but your son's expressionless, non-response to you suggests secrecy, and maybe a mischievous intent. You press harder, but he remains silent. Not because he has something specific to hide, but because he feels he has nothing to share. "How can this be?" the parent thinks, "Why doesn't he see the urgency of the situation?"

The simple truth is many boys don't think of forgetfulness or the misplacing of homework as events worth reporting or getting upset about. In fact, talking about such failings makes them feel bad. This explains one of their core beliefs: "if we don't talk about it, then it's not

Inside the world of professional psychology, therapists sometimes refer to the "magical thinking" of boys. Some boys seem to think they can make a problem disappear by refusing to acknowledge it. Magical thinking is a habit of concern at age 14, but can be a crisis at age 18 — when magical thinking can lead to believing that education or apprenticeship is irrelevant to your future!

a problem." Or, "let's not waste time talking about trivial stuff, because it distracts me from more important things. I don't care if you're upset about the state of my sock drawer." In general, we need to talk about more serious, interesting things if we want to hold boys' attention.

Although a refusal to communicate is likely to create tension, it doesn't necessarily mean that boys have something to hide. Rather than harboring secrets, the boundaries boys draw have more to do with their inclination to stake out private mental space, which among other things, allows them to relax and think more clearly. Boys, like adults, typically have a set of private rules for who gets to enter their mental space, and which topics are open and closed for discussion. In my experience, there is a gender issue here. Mothers, more than fathers, seem intent on discovering the reason why boys want to remain private. This pursuit may come from a place of love and concern, but doesn't necessarily translate that way for boys. Even more important is that there is usually little to be discovered. Most of the time, resistance to talking reflects awkwardness, minor embarrassment, or sheer cluelessness about what to say. Such awkwardness can even shape the atmosphere of a casual car ride with a boy between 9 and 15.

"It's Stressful to Let You In"

We should understand that boys' impetus to defend their mental space is not only to protect privacy, but also because it feels so stressful to open up their mental space or orbit to others. If you are a social person who enjoys connecting with others, this may sound ridiculous. But for boys generally, it's a fact of life. Many dread having to open up enough that others can know, and possibly judge, their thoughts. This defensiveness is not consistent. There are times when boys enjoy connecting, and there are amazing and honest conversations that go on between friends and family. But even among peers, sharing is more easily prompted by a desire to express opinions or convey swagger than an interest in being close.

Personal communication is particularly stressful because it requires a degree of *mental clarity that is a scarce resource for many boys*. To invite people into your mental space means you are prepared to be clear and open about your thoughts. That sort of laser focus is a stretch for most boys, and given a choice, they'd rather be caught up in their own thoughts and reflections. Boys have a strong tendency toward day-dreaming, and that includes allowing their mind to construct a variety of images, both fantasy and reality. The content of that collage varies by age, and is somewhat unique to the individual. As satisfying as these personal interests might be, it's not the same as thinking in words, or more complete thoughts. I don't mean to get too abstract here, it's just that for many boys there is a strong nonverbal element to their thoughts (images, songs, visual memories). When that's the case, you can imagine how hard it is to shift gears to start relating in words. Accordingly, a primary question for many boys is: "why do adults talk so much?"

The images and reflections that occupy boys' minds aren't necessarily formed into a coherent or complete idea. When others want to know what's on their mind, it requires that they provide a sensible account of what they're thinking about. That can be stressful or embarrassing; boys often feel a little silly about the content of their imaginations. They also feel embarrassed when they realize that others have noticed how deeply caught up they are in their own thoughts and emotions. Being observed having strong emotions (other than anger or humor) is a point of sensitivity and discomfort for many boys. Strong feelings suggest a degree of vulnerability, and that is an unwanted association for older boys especially.

"Talking Makes Me Feel Vulnerable"

We've examined some of the reasons that communication makes boys feel uncomfortable. I believe the best word to describe this discomfort is vulnerability. Here, I'm referring to an emotional state in which a person feels as though they are too exposed — like their thoughts and emotions are an open book to others. There are two basic dimensions to this issue. First, social communication is a window to boy's emotions and inner life. Many boys fear that the more they talk, the more exposed they will be, and the more they will be misinterpreted. Second, there is anxiety about *others seeing and judging the way that they think*. Boys may be particularly anxious about others seeing the difficulties they have in knowing their own minds — "I can't explain what I'm thinking and feeling." That anxiety goes even higher in quiet settings, conducive to intimate conversation. Too much quiet adds drama and self-consciousness. Some boys never outgrow this problem — even as they become husbands, parents, coaches, and employees.

> Boys may privately feel sure of themselves, and what they think. But that doesn't mean they can articulate themselves well enough to demonstrate their intelligence or perspective. This leads to self-consciousness and a feeling of vulnerability. It's a natural human instinct to hunker down and protect that vulnerability, and boys do that by talking less and opting out of ambiguous social interactions — like when they're going to be asked questions for which they have no clear answers.

The most important thing we can do if we want to increase boys' conversational courage is to minimize the vulnerability they feel. In Part Two of this book we will be looking at helping to manage vulnerability. For now, try to notice signs of vulnerability in your interactions with boys. Silence, and a lack of eye contact are two prominent indications of vulnerability. It's also important to listen for signals in the way that boys talk. For example, changes in the prosody of their speech, like the pitch, rhythm, and tone, will alert you to changes in their emotions. Each child has his own way of converting stress into changes in speech and behavior — that includes acting silly, regressed, or dismissive. These are all prospective indications of vulnerability. I'm specifically referring to fear and apprehension, and the idea that "opening up for conversation puts me in a one down position because you're much better at talking than me."

Oh, and when all else fails, boys are famous for using indignation as an emotional defense. Anxiety morphs into personal offense, "how dare you try to invade my privacy with these ridiculous questions!" "Don't you respect me?" "You don't have a right to ask me that." So begins a parent-child debate worthy of a supreme court hearing. When this happens, step back and agree with his perspective. Your agreement erases the notion that the two of you are on different sides. Then, begin to talk about less touchy topics that are more likely to instill confidence than fear. Conversations about sensitive topics should unfold slowly, ensuring a sense of safety. Too often, our own adult anxiety prompts us to get right to the point with boys, which only makes them dig in deeper.

#2 — You're Trying to Control Me

Boys think in basic categories like who's in charge, and who's the subordinate. It's a maddening tendency because it oversimplifies relationships and situations, often leading to distortions that make boys feel unnecessarily weak or controlled by others. The effects of this way of thinking are worse when there has been a history of conflict, like frequent arguments, anger, yelling, and unresolved differences. When we adults have conflicts with kids we may get frustrated, but realize that our age gives us authority, and relatively more control. Kids are also frustrated by conflict, and for them there's the added awareness that the situation is largely out of their control. The net result can be a terse communication style, sometimes marked by half-truths. For example:

"Your brother says you hit him, is that true?"
"No."
"Then why would he say that?"
"I don't know."
"He says you pushed him on the floor, and his knee's red."
"Yeah."
"Well I just asked if you if you hit him!"
"I pushed him, I didn't hit him. Why do you always take his side and make stuff up? You never believe me."

This sort of blockheadedness can quickly get interpreted as oppositional when the boy's actual underlying motive is fear. Boys tend to believe that talking will get them cornered. They may try to say as little as possible so as not to offer up something sensitive that they can't defend later. As adults, we can get annoyed by a minimal effort, which feels like withholding or oppositionality. This can make for some circular conversations in which we feel foolish for pursuing a topic in the first place. In such cases, boys often discover their "inner lawyer," taking delight in challenging adult logic as a way of asserting their own authority.

The closing argument will surely underscore the ridiculousness of any directive or inquiry we might have intended to make.

A big part of resisting control is not wanting to feel like a subordinate. Dividing the world into winners and losers leads boys to feel like losers when we demand answers to interrogation-like questions. Their defiance in these situations is often misunderstood as an intent to be aggravating or deliberately oppositional. But the real drama in these types of interactions is the way that communication makes boys feel small and ineffectual. Requiring boys to respond in a submissive manner robs them of dignity, and from that unhappy disposition they will surely try to make our lives miserable in return! The bottom line is that no one likes to feel like they are the lesser half of a conversation or relationship. We can avoid this sort of mess by remaining respectful, even as we raise difficult topics, or issue a directive. We can begin by using the right vocal tone, and strategic eye contact (see Chapter 5).

The Hidden Fear of Being Controlled

Boys are wary of where a conversation is headed when questions are framed with an irritated or anxious tone. For example, are you maneuvering to catch them in a lie? Are you jockeying to get them to admit to something that they have denied for a long time? Are you deliberately trying to confuse them so that they end up looking foolish? I'm not describing a clinical level of paranoia, but elements of fearful thinking can stem from a deep self-absorption. Essentially, a boy can be so deep into his own thoughts, worries, and opinions that he starts believing the questions or comments of others are an intentional effort to assault the fortress of his own mind. Once this suspicion sets in, it becomes increasingly difficult to connect because the boy meets every step forward with an escalated defense. This can be manifest as a refusal to respond, answering every question with a question of his own, or a plain old angry outburst.

Many years ago, when psychology was first becoming a science, theories were advanced about the building blocks of personality. Some of these theories are still useful, and one clarifies the psychology of males, and their need to be in control. I'm referring to a theory from the prominent psychologist Alfred Adler, who developed what he called the Number-One Priority model of personality.[11] Basically, Adler said that every personality is dominated by one of four different priorities: Pleasing, Comfort, Moral Superiority, or Control. The important thing to understand is that Adler believed an individual's personality developed to compensate (or hide) a person's greatest vulnerability, or fear. Accordingly, Adler explained that a *Pleasing* personality was an attempt to compensate for a fear of rejection. Basically, *Comfort*-oriented personalities tend to fear stress. These individuals really dislike conflict, and would rather hold back their opinions than risk an angry argument. They often lack ambition — perhaps preferring hours of games on the couch to other more goal-directed activities. *Morally Superior* personalities dread meaninglessness. For them, every choice or action should be associated with some important meaning. So, dinner is not merely supper and sustenance, it's an opportunity to break bread with kindred spirits, and have a deep conversation.

Adler's fourth type is a *Control* personality. This person is shaped by fear of humiliation and embarrassment and will go to any length to avoid those possibilities. In my experience, the Control priority is common among males of all ages; Adler's description of this type helps us to understand at a deeper level why it is that boys need to control conversation. Many boys live in fear and suspicion that talking increases the likelihood they will be embarrassed. So, they work diligently to control the frequency of talking and what is spoken about. It's a way of dealing with underlying fear.

Unfortunately, on the surface, boys' efforts to control are often expressed as anger and belligerence. How are we supposed to communicate with these boys? What is the best way to minimize their feelings of fear and vulnerability?

The most effective thing we can do to increase conversational courage is to minimize boy's vulnerability while talking. For example, begin conversations with topics they enjoy and know a lot about. Move while talking, like taking a walk, playing catch, or taking a ride in the car. The basic idea is to relieve tension and stress. Motion really helps.

#3 — You're Boring

Reality check. Like it or not, boys often find adults boring. I know it's hard to accept, and I know we don't feel boring. With their conviction that adults are boring, boys can minimize the importance of what we say. As a rule, if it isn't immediately stimulating, and of clear personal relevance to boys, it's a boring topic. For example, perseverating about responsibilities and character ranks high on the "boring barometer" — unless you link those qualities to attributes, like strength and honor, that boys covet. Some boys feel no inhibition about thinking we are boring, and are more than happy to bluntly share their perspective. Others try to hide these feelings, worrying that they will be perceived as disrespectful. Usually, however, their nonverbal indicators betray them. It's painfully obvious when boys are bored. For example: little eye contact, expressionless face, dismissive mumbling, restlessness, yawning.

How did we get so boring? Practice, practice, practice. *We repeat ourselves all the time. We rely on familiar phrases that seem poignant to us, but which bore anyone born in this century half to death.* It comes down to this: if you serve up frequent reminders too frequently, you'll eventually be tuned out. Boys will correctly conclude they've heard it before. You may be thinking "I know I've said this before, but you're still not responding — you must not hear me." Ah, but he does hear you, and he's concluded that what you talk about is dull and irritating. When we're addressing themes of great importance, we naturally want to emphasize key aspects. We want to feel assured that kids understand what we're talking about. Yet from a boy's perspective, such reiteration is redundant, unnecessary, and ultimately a snooze.

In some ways, I don't like making these assertions because they can sound insulting and hurtful. But my job — indeed my career — has been focused on decoding the psychology and behavior of boys. So, I'm serving up what I believe to be the truth, even if it's painful to acknowledge. In consolation, let me add this isn't the end of the story. In Part II, I will be covering themes and perspectives that I have found to be of high relevance to boys, and which help build the bridges between adults and boys that many of us hope for.

"So What Have I Done Wrong Now?"

The tedium boys feel when communicating with adults is further heightened when they feel as though they're always being told about something that they've done wrong. Boys may believe — sometimes justifiably — that the only reason a parent wants their attention is because the boy has made a mistake. If they are chronically reluctant to communicate, boys are partially responsible for this unfortunate situation. We can challenge their negative expectations by surprising boys with compliments and other forms of affirmation.

Sometimes, if they anticipate a problem or reprimand, it seems boys are baiting us to emphasize negative messages. Best strategy: surprise them with a positive comment, compliment, or question that affirms respect for their knowledge.

For example, a sour look and tone go a long way in souring communication. If we take the bait, announcing an endless list of problems when we do have boys' attention, we will have reinforced their worst expectations of adults. At moments when you do have something negative to say or talk about, it's best to preface it by talking about something of mutual interest that promotes a sense of friendliness and openness, rather than judgment.

"The Most Interesting Subject Is Me"

We've already touched upon the self-absorption of boys and how it affects their working memory. But self-absorption also affects their sense of priorities. Understand that there is a hierarchy that boys use in determining what is most important. At the top of this hierarchy are topics of great personal interest. For younger boys, this typically revolves around interesting tasks. For older boys, aspects of self-development take on special interest. When we're not talking about these kinds of things, we can be perceived as being boring or irrelevant. For the most part, this is not a judgment about your character. Instead, it's a critique of what you are saying.

If you can get past frustration with boys for being so self-absorbed, you can use their inherent interest in their own lives to jumpstart great conversations. Spend lots of time asking about their opinions and interests. Recognize that at those moment when boys seem to have nothing to say, they are processing all kind of thoughts, ideas, and worries of personal relevance. You can "set the table" for great conversations, which includes making the situations feel safe for boys. I will be discussing these strategies in detail in Part II.

#4 — You're Confusing

A common obstacle for boys is that they don't quickly enough get the point of what an adult is saying. In other words, they may be thinking "why don't you just say what you mean?" This is especially likely when we offer a long preamble to the point that we want to make. Consequently, boys feel confused: what is he talking about? The best approach is to chunk information so that boys can digest your idea in a logical, orderly way. Much of the difficulty here involves boys' difficulty following the flow of conversation and the nuances of a social idea. For example, boys may not appreciate that a preamble is necessary to set the tone for the point that an adult wants to make. In addition, unnecessarily complex words make important points unnecessarily complex.

What I'm *not* saying here is that you should "dumb down" what you want to say. Being clear is good, but oversimplifying feels condescending and alienates even very young boys. It is critical that we take young people seriously, and convey that regard in our tone and expressions.

Confusion may also come if we forget the point of what we want to say. When we talk with other adults we can count on them to "read between the lines" of our thoughts and words. They know how adults think and express themselves, and can appreciate that one minute we

When we're talking to boys, it's helpful to think of ourselves as narrating our thoughts. This reminds us to express our thoughts in a clear and logical manner. Narrating clarifies, and it feels friendly and sociable. It helps boys feel more confident in responding.

are talking about a friend and the next we may be referring to ourselves, without officially stating that the subject of conversation has changed. Boys are much less skilled about sensing and understanding these conversational transitions.

"Why Are You Looking at Me Like That?"

Another source of confusion during communication is nonverbal cues and, specifically, the facial expressions that we use with boys. If we adopt a look of concern, it has a way of unnerving kids. They may feel as though our sympathy is a sign that they've done something wrong, or something bad has happened for which they should feel badly. If we can remember that our own nonverbal communication is saying much more than our words, we can use nonverbal signals strategically. Most boys become adept at reading small signals in our facial expressions, and we need to be careful that these signals don't contradict our words.

Remember

- Before asking a question, think about how you would feel if your son posed the same question, in the same tone.
- Boredom is the enemy of a positive connection. Be honest and straightforward. Talk about serious things.
- Don't get offended by boys' assertion of privacy. Personal boundaries are less about keeping secrets than having control of personal mental space.

Points to Consider

- What emotions are you conveying with your tone and facial expressions?
- Are you remembering to move while talking?
- Are you remembering to come up for air while making an important point?
- Have you accepted that the things that are most important to you may be of much less importance to boys? Do you recognize this is natural, and that overcoming this divide requires time and effort?

Chapter 4

Great Beginnings

G ETTING A GREAT CONVERSATION going requires heightened awareness, and an understanding of how to respond to what you perceive. Self-awareness alone doesn't guarantee a connection, but a great connection is virtually impossible without it. There's something about paying close attention to your tone and attitude that goes a long way toward building rapport. By rapport, I mean projecting respect and interest in another person. Sometimes people think rapport is simply a matter of being charismatic — as though great conversations are the same thing as a great sales pitch on the showroom floor of your local automobile dealership. Marketing gurus like to portray effective sales pitches as "conversations," but that's just wishful thinking. A real conversation implies authentic connection to know someone better, rather than trying to sell them something.

Respect is the key, and figuring out how to *project* respect is a practical concern. I'm not trying to say that you should genuflect in front of boys, or somehow be submissive. Respect does not always mean showing deference. Confusion about this issue is a common mistake in our society, causing lots of people to withhold respect. There is, for many, a false assumption that giving respect implies one is of lower status, or subordinate. When I talk about giving respect, I'm referring to holding another person in full regard. This means perceiving the whole of that person: words, expression, body language, and tone — all the things that make up that person's presence. To respect someone, you must be willing to take in the breadth of their being — even during awkwardness or anger. I realize you may be thinking this sounds too formal or unnatural with respect to the conversations you've had with boys. But sustained awareness of yourself as a communicator allows respect to flow, and that builds closeness.

Establishing the fundamental necessity of respect is only the price of admission to great conversation. You still need some core strategies for developing a good connection. In this chapter, I'm going to address specific strategies for getting conversations off to a great start. Try not to interpret these strategies in a programmatic, stiff way. In other words, don't imagine yourself with a checklist, needing to tick off each strategy. You might need only one or a few. At times, some will undoubtedly be more useful to you than others. Many of these strategies have been helpful to me in my clinical office, and I have been teaching these approaches to those who want to better connect with boys for many years.

Avoid the Kitchen Table

Place is an important consideration in getting things off to a good start. Various places in your home may have certain emotional associations for kids, and I think it best to avoid places that have strong associations with being lectured, scolded, or worried. The kitchen table is one such place. In many ways, it is a key site of stress at home. It is both a place that a child does his homework, and where he receives stern talks about mistakes, or possibly some type of warning. Don't let the kitchen table trap you or your son. When you sit down around a table there is often a heavy feeling that sets in for boys, causing them to put up emotional defenses. It's better to vary the places that you have conversations with boys so that there isn't one place that they consistently associate with the feeling of "OK, here we go again." Hint: a much better, more productive place to have a conversation is driving together in the car, for reasons that we will discuss in Chapter 5.

Make *Your* Point

Parents often worry that if they are too direct in talking to boys that it will backfire, causing boys to feel overwhelmed, possibly inciting anger. In most cases, avoidance of your main point is a mistake. Conversation is likely to be both more comfortable and manageable when you are clear about what you want from a conversation. It is certainly helpful to do a little relationship building before jumping into a stressful topic, but boys don't like conversations that meander. Some conversation is more casual and spontaneous, but here I'm talking about starting a conversation that has a specific focus or goal. In such cases, the tone you adopt will make all the difference — and we'll get into this in depth in the next chapter. For now, the important thing to remember is not to be afraid of expressing expectations prior to beginning a conversation. *Expressing expectations* is a way of giving conversation a purpose. Then, any questions you might ask are posed about that purpose. In my clinical family work, parents often hedge in asking what they want to know, which then causes boys to answer in vague, unproductive terms. Some of the mental games that adolescent boys play in response to parental inquiries stem from parents' obfuscation. It may appear that boys are being evasive, but before we assume a devious intention we should ask ourselves whether they understand the main point we are making. Without such clarification boys may wonder how their answers will be understood, and possibly used against them. Ambiguity may be effective in a police interrogation; a detective may have the right to demand answers to questions without explaining why they are being asked. But in families and schools we should aspire to create a different atmosphere, and project a degree of respect not required during an interrogation. By saying you want to understand why it's been difficult to shut down the electronics and get to bed on time, then questions have a pragmatic foundation. There is no hidden meaning, and the intention to solve an important problem is made clear. *Declaration of intent* is also an important element of honesty and humility — factors which propel closeness and a constructive outcome.

Begin With *His* Expertise

Sometimes the point of a conversation is not to explore a specific topic, but to spend time relating. When in doubt about what to say or where to begin, always defer to topics that a person already knows a lot about — areas where he can feel like an expert. It's useful to adopt this approach when the situation feels awkward, or you're at a loss for words. This might occur when it's been a long time since the last good talk. Conversely, it might be at a time when there is a more sensitive topic to be addressed, but which you don't want to bring up until you've established some rapport and trust. At these times, it's best to begin by asking questions about topics on which boys have a lot to say. Naturally, this varies from one child to the next, but there's always something about which he has enough knowledge that he can do a significant share of the talking. Sometimes, I rely on what I know is a younger boy's favorite cartoon or television show. Other times I turn to sports or friendships.

What's important is to create a sense of comfort and confidence, which can in turn help boys to do their share of the talking. For me, it's important to detect that boys are getting comfortable with the sound of their own voice, explaining things to me. The explaining part is very important. Rather than just asking for opinions, I try to ask about things that need to be explained because they involve a significant level of complexity. For example, I don't just want to know that a boy has gotten a new laptop, I want to know what type of laptop it is, what features it has, and how he came to choose it. I want to know more than what he's reading, but which parts of the book he found interesting, and why.

During such conversation starters make sure not to pass judgment, or inadvertently signal that you're judging or questioning his ideas. Instead, be an attentive listener and allow his commentary to lead you to the next question. There will be times when boys resist, fearing that it will only lead to topics which they find more uncomfortable. With younger boys, when I'm struggling to get a conversation started and it seems that every topic is a dead end, I sometimes revert to a world of sensory experience. This may sound silly to you, but when I'm really stuck I ask about food choices. Would you rather eat chicken fingers or mac n' cheese? Usually I can get a response to that basic question, which leads me to my next question: would you choose a pizza and salad or fish and chips? This approach may sound slightly absurd, and I'm a bit self-conscious in sharing it with you! Yet embedded in this apparently silly question is an invitation to make increasingly complex choices about food combinations. *It's not the answers that are important — it's the feeling of being asked such questions which builds an amicable relationship.* Often, I keep quizzing on these sorts of choices, which in almost every case delights boys. There is something playful and affectionate about this way of connecting with kids, and I bet it will work for you as well. It may seem like I'm quizzing about something trivial. However, remember that food preferences are extremely important to children. This is a special subset of knowledge, and it is a constant point of reference in their lives. Food is one of the most important choices boys make. Knowing your favorite foods, and your personal hierarchy of favorites, is a part of knowing yourself well.

Tempo and Relaxation

Strategic tempo complements an emphasis on expertise. It might seem counterintuitive, but a quick tempo at the outset of conversation is often relaxing for boys. A rapid tempo seems to match the pace and rhythm of their own thought (like how their thoughts tend to bounce from one topic to another). You can help this tempo materialize in your conversations by touching upon a variety of topics. For example, I might begin by asking somebody about their day in school, but then rapidly move on to asking who they sat with at lunch and what they talked about, and then what they're going to do after therapy, and then what they thought of an important event that happened during the past week, and so on. Each of these questions is asked in a matter-of-fact, direct way, allowing relatively little time for reflection. *At this point, the answers are less important than establishing tempo-based rapport.*

A matter-of-fact tempo that moves quickly from one topic to the next feels natural and relaxing to boys — even if it feels the opposite to us. You may believe that this is not true. Maybe you've seen boys that are more relaxed if you talk slowly, and give them ample time to respond. I agree this can be true, *but not so much at the outset of a conversation.* Remember that we're talking about great beginnings and how to get a conversation going. When we reflect on the value of staying calm, and thinking more deeply about what boys say, that approach is better suited to interactions that are further along the conversation time line. At the outset of conversation, it's useful to simply get things moving.

A tempo that matches the natural speed of thought, including the way that thoughts and ideas ricochet within the mind, feels natural to most boys. It's an approach that comes across as friendly.

Do Something Together

Movement is one of your best allies in helping boys to relax, and getting them to communicate more openly. Movement directs attention toward what is happening in the body, rather than isolating attention to what is happening in the mind. When people are intensely stressed they are almost always living from the neck up, forgetting their bodies, and forgetting how activity and exertion can relax the mind. Most boys are *naturally energetic beings who feel more comfortable with themselves when their bodies are in motion.* Take advantage of this natural inclination. For example, play a game of catch, take a walk, do a chore, attend to an animal; even playing a simple board game involves some degree of motor movement that can potentially reduce stress. Sometimes you can use the speed of an activity to promote a lively conversation. For example, speeding up your pace when taking a walk is a good way to generate more energy, and a more spirited conversation. By extension, slowing your body down is effective in encouraging reflection, and perhaps deeper insight.

Movement can also fill awkward silences. Two people playing catch will continue to play even when neither can think of something to say. The game of catch maintains the relationship during moments of silence and reflection. It's important not to lose focus during those silences because there's still a lot of mental activity going on, and both people may be thinking about things that have not been said. In this way, movement allows you to bear witness to a person's emotional process without feeling as though you must be constantly talking to be an active participant. Many times, I've initiated a game of catch with boys in my office as a way of getting them to open up, and then allowed them to do most of the talking. If it feels like conversation is sluggish, I pick up the tempo. If the game becomes so raucous that it interferes with relating, I slow things down. With older boys, I sometimes take a walk. In each case, it seems important to let movement and motion create more fluency in conversation — even when the words aren't working exactly as you hoped they might.

Include an Animal

Setting the stage for great communication means paying attention to context. Sometimes, it's helpful to triangulate the conversation. Typically, triangulation is a negative term with respect to psychotherapy, and especially family psychotherapy. It describes how two people can oppose and outnumber the third person, or how two people might avoid working a problem out because a third party is involved. Ah, but when the third party is an animal, triangulation takes on a noticeably different quality. An animal can serve as a safe and neutral source of support for boys. The warmth and texture of an animal's coat is reassuring, providing tactile physical comfort from a source of unconditional affection. It's difficult to overstate the benefits of animals. Even when two people are at odds, they tend to experience a common sense of empathy for the animal, which then makes it easier for those two people to explore their empathy for each other. A dog's behavior in such a situation usually demonstrates that it loves both people, allowing for mutual positive regard. I do almost all therapy with a dog present. My dog, Darcy, is not officially a therapy dog, but over the years she has intuitively understood her role as a provider of comfort and reassurance in psychotherapy sessions. Her warmth is both physical and spiritual, and I depend on her as I would any close colleague. I have a strong belief in the benefits dogs offer humans, but I also believe that the presence of a lizard, frog, or aquarium can be of benefit. I have learned from my own research that boys would feel much more comfortable in virtually any school if there were various kinds of animals, simply walking around and socializing with everyone! This may sound absurd, but only to those who have not spent time working with kids, and who haven't yet seen the powerful effect of animals in school settings. In your own private conversations with boys, put this power to use: include an animal. You can both spend some time addressing and touching the animal before more formal conversation begins.

Inquire Before You Assume

While it is helpful to spend time thinking about what you want to say before beginning a conversation, be careful not to get so far ahead in your thoughts that you assume you know what the child or adolescent is thinking, or feeling. Inquiring is a basic element of respect, and it keeps conversations vital and in the present. As soon as you start building an argument around assumptions, others can sense that the conversation has been scripted; this is when boys tend to tune out. This is natural. Doesn't it feel a little bit like being cornered when you're forced into a conversation that has been pre-scripted to make you look wrong and another person look right? Begin with genuine inquiry. Remain open-minded and flexible, responding to what is said. Ask real questions and avoid assuming you know how they will be answered. When building a relationship is high priority, it's almost always better to ask more questions, and do less pontificating or lecturing. Try not to come across as the "all-knowing" voice of authority. Be a partner in conversation, which means showing willingness to spend as much time listening as talking.

By making this assertion I don't mean to imply that adults should have no more authority than young people. To the contrary, I am a strong believer in the need for parents to be authoritative. However, I also understand that parents who rely too heavily on assumptions may lose the openness that authentic questions convey, and thus lose the sincerity that makes connection with boys more meaningful. An important reason for remaining flexible and open-minded is that the thinking of boys tends to be idiosyncratic. Not only do their perspectives reflect unique aspects of their personality, but also unique interpretations of various situations. When it comes to judging the behavior of boys, we may be challenged to separate our judgment of the behavior from the thinking that spurred the behavior. In other words, *a person can be wrong in their actions but may have made that choice with legitimate concerns or anxieties in mind.* When we want to correct behavior, we're better off empathizing with the thinking and emotions that precipitated those actions, before we rush to judge and reprimand poor choices.

Be Relaxed, Look Relaxed

If you are feeling so agitated that you have something you must get off your chest — and you want to talk about it now, I encourage you to rethink your options. It's probably the wrong time to talk — the wrong time to start relating. Your agitation or anxiety will show on your face and in your body language. More likely than not, it will cause a boy to tighten up, and be unconstructively guarded. Feeling vulnerable always causes one to be guarded, and that's exactly the opposite of what you want to create in building a great relationship. On the other hand, if you're relaxed, it won't seem that anything bad is about to happen. You project no sense of doom, no immediate sense of worry.

Many of the strategies recommended in this chapter cannot be effectively accomplished if you're in an agitated, anxious state. And it's not enough to be relaxed; *you should also look relaxed.* That's because your appearance and nonverbal communication are the primary ways that the boy will interpret your mental state. People who are anxious often have a more constricted or rigid expression. Rather than flowing with the conversation, their minds are preoccupied with worry about the past or future. They seem to be everywhere but the present. Agitation or anxiety may also cause us to cut other people off, rather than letting them finish their point. Instead, make it your practice to consciously hang back, giving boys enough time to make their point before you interject a counterpoint or correction. Speak slowly because the pace of your speech also conveys the degree of your attention. Earlier, we spoke about using a rapid tempo because it feels friendly and conversational. However, if you find that you are agitated or anxious, it's best to practice a different strategy, and that means slowing down.

Talk Slightly Above His Age

The last point I want to make in this list is perhaps the least obvious. It involves conveying respect and being interesting. My suggestion is that you try to talk slightly above the age of the boy you are addressing. When we do, it makes our ideas or argument just a little more complex than what boys might be anticipating, and that's more interesting. On countless occasions, I have listened to parents simplify an idea to an extent that it's at least a little condescending — and boys are quick to show their embarrassment or irritation.

That parental instinct comes from a place of concern but often backfires. It's good for boys to wrangle with ideas that are slightly more sophisticated or multifaceted than what they are accustomed to. Accordingly, using a vocabulary that's one to two years above a boy's age invites him to think about people and situations with greater appreciation for situational and psychological complexity. This helps to make learning more exciting and privileged. Almost everyone enjoys being brought inside the inner workings of a problem or situation, where he is invited to ponder questions of substance and consequence. That's what it feels like when someone respects you enough to confide advanced thoughts or questions. Naturally, we should be careful not to be confusing, or use words that are a mystery to boys. That would be the opposite of everything I'm suggesting in this book. We also don't want to go too far and start thinking of younger boys as adults, confiding in them the way we would a peer or spouse. There is a degree of subtlety in this strategy, but I believe when it's used creatively, and when it comes from a place of positive regard for boys, it raises the conversation's level of seriousness. The corresponding shift in tone is itself inviting and encouraging. This is one important way of making a lasting, positive first impression.

Remember

- Getting off to a good start "sets the table" for a constructive conversation. The approach you use should be guided by the situation at hand.
- Respect always promotes trust and greater openness. Your honesty and humility are primary ways of modeling respect. In this way, conversations are a teaching opportunity.

Points to Consider

- How well is your tempo working? Does it match the topic at hand, and the emotions involved?
- Would the inclusion of movement or an animal be helpful?
- Is this a conversation that needs greater clarity, or more relationship building?
- Are you keeping the conversation interesting by talking a little above his age?

Chapter 5

Vocal Tone and Eye Contact

W HEN PEOPLE SAY THEY ARE STRUGGLING TO COMMUNICATE with their sons or male students, my suspicion is that they are paying too much attention to words, and not enough to signals. A question is asked with words, but the importance of the question, and the feelings of the asker, are conveyed by signals like vocal tone and eye contact. Before boys can even hear your words — before their brains ever sort out the word meaning of what you're saying — they are listening to the tone of your speech. Please try to fully absorb this concept, because it can change everything about your approach. Accepting this reality will spare you frustration, and in many cases, will save you time.

Generally, we should think of communication as having both *form* and *content*. Most people get caught up in the *content* (the words) and forget the powerful effect of *form* (your voice and other nonverbal signals). It is with your eyes and voice that you set the table for a great conversation, orienting boys to listen deeply and respond well.

In this chapter, I'll explain how to use your vocal tone and eyes in a way that feels comforting and encouraging to boys. I want to help you shape your communication so that you can gain their full attention, and feel confident that you are connecting. You'll find that the idea is straightforward and sensible. Don't be fooled, however, into believing that simply understanding these ideas will be all that's needed. You will need to practice in the ways I suggest, and you'll need to get comfortable with the idea that every interaction includes preparing its *presentation*. Basically, you need to think about the ways your voice and eyes are being read, and you'll have to consciously work at presenting those signals in a constructive way. As you gain confidence and skill using nonverbal signals, you'll find that you become more effective at leading conversations, and more confident in creating closeness. As a parent, teacher, or coach, knowing how to use these skills will allow you to convey important content much more effectively. That is our goal, and I'm going to help you increase the frequency of your success.

Vocal Tone

Let's start with the most basic and useful signal of all: vocal tone. Each of us can use vocal tone as a means of connecting, and being more clearly heard. Even though you create tone with your voice, tone itself is not strictly verbal. It has do with the sound of your voice, especially the pitch, timbre, and rhythm of your speech. These elements or signals of speech are formally called prosody. The *prosody*, or tone of your communication, is the primary way you convey your emotional state to others. Sometimes that is not intentional, but make no mistake, it's the tone that reveals your state of mind every time. *Learn to control tone, and you will have learned how to shape the impression you leave with others.*

Tone is how boys understand what sort of conversation they are about to have. This is not a conscious choice on their part, but it is inevitable because it's so much easier for a person to perceive and make sense of nonverbal signals like tone. Think about this for just a moment. If you are in conversation with a good friend, you're much more likely to notice the pitch of her voice, or the speed of his speech, before you comprehend the meaning of her words, just a second later. So, what's the big deal about a microsecond's delay? Well, that short delay enables our brains to make remarkable interpretations about the speaker. Once you've detected the tone and rhythm of communication, you can't ignore it. You've been primed to interpret the words in a particular way. If your friend is speaking quickly, in a frantic pitch, it will almost certainly be difficult for him to convince you that he is calm, and in no rush. This is just human nature. We are all taking in nonverbal signals all the time, and we're using that information to paint a more complete mental picture of what the other person is thinking or feeling — and more specifically — what they are thinking or feeling about us.

Because boys sometimes struggle with verbal nuances, such as understanding the meaning of words (especially when they are used metaphorically or in unfamiliar ways), they naturally pay more attention to tone. Those signals are a lifeline to what is going on in the here and now. And when they feel confused about what the tone of your voice is conveying, they might scan your face, paying special attention to your eyes as a way of determining your attitude and intention. Sometimes there are contradictions. For example, just because you proclaim, "it's fine, I'm not angry," doesn't mean that is the same message your voice and eyes convey.

Our task as adults is to harness the power of tone as a means of creating a strong and meaningful connection with boys. When we do this well, we are acting as a coach, encouraging and guiding a child to reciprocate. Coaches need a variety of strategies to be effective teachers, and so we benefit from having at least a couple of different vocal tones to rely upon. The more masterfully we manage those tones, the better chance we have of creating a productive atmosphere for conversation. If you're paying close attention to a significant boy in your life, I'm sure you will notice that some approaches consistently work better than others. You'll begin to discover that there is an optimal atmosphere for talking, and you will eventually sense how your face and voice help to create that atmosphere.

Activating Safety and Trust

Let me emphasize, your voice is the single most powerful tool you have in establishing positive, safe connections with boys. Safety and trust are essential because they enable boys, and men for that matter, to get past their sense of vulnerability. You might imagine that there are all kinds of vocal tones to accomplish this goal. But when it comes to boys, there is one type or direction of tone that proves more effective than others for most. The essence of this tone, which we might think of as a *task-tone*, is to be *matter-of-fact* — and slightly *monotone*. A somewhat monotone, matter-of-fact voice removes unhelpful emotions from the challenge of connecting and being heard. A task-tone makes it easier for boys to pay attention to the substance of what you want to say. It does this by eliminating counterproductive signals from your voice and attitude. Those signals — like a pitch that conveys worry, or a pace that suggests irritation — add layers of complexity which may unintentionally heighten a boy's sense of vulnerability.

Imagine that you need to talk to your son about a serious mistake he has made; perhaps there have been some unfortunate, embarrassing consequences. Using a high level of emotion in your voice signals your son to feel upset because you are upset. On an emotional level this may feel gratifying, and on an intellectual level it may feel honest, but it's not constructive in getting to the bottom of the matter. An exchange begun with high emotion ultimately pivots around tension and the strong, disconcerting emotion being expressed, rather than the facts. But aren't adults entitled to have emotions when talking to boys? Absolutely, that is your right, and there may be moments in life when it's simply not appropriate to hide those emotions. What I'm talking about, however, are day-to-day challenges of conversing effectively with kids who shut down in the face of such emotions.

By emphasizing task-tone, I'm recommending that you initiate conversation using a voice that enables boys to clearly hear the content of what you are saying. You must trust this suggestion, because it works almost every time. Now, I know that some readers will think to themselves, "my son or student is more sophisticated; he's capable of verbal nuance, he uses larger words, and communicates with sophisticated syntax." That may be true, but if you use the vocal tone I'm recommending, the boy in question will find it even easier to process the content of what you want to say. My work with boys has taken me to many cities and different countries, and *even in the most cosmopolitan places, with highly intelligent kids, I use task-tone to make a trusted connection*, and it inevitably does.

It's true that boys are ultimately responsible for learning to decode all kinds of human vocal tones, and each of us will surely use a variety of tones in our communication with boys. Yet the foundation of a good relationship, and an excellent entry point into great conversation, is to use a matter-of-fact, workman-like tone. It's this tone that resonates with the instincts of boys, especially their desire for economy of expression and a clear outcome. A task-tone gently relaxes any apprehension they might have about talking. Creating your personal version of task-tone will require experimentation. Specifically, you must learn to communicate in shorter sentences. Be succinct. Avoid making too much eye contact when you want boys to dedicate their attention to content. Remember, your goal is to create a conversational atmosphere that relaxes your child so that it's easier for him to process the basic ideas of what you are saying. It can be hard to remember this at times when you're feeling upset, rushed, or irritable. At such times, step back and think about the nonverbal aspects of your message before you start communicating. Generally, it's better not to start difficult or sensitive conversations when your primary intention is to vent. (Many certainly know this from experience in their primary relationship.) You may feel better after such a conversation, but it's unlikely that your son will. Those sorts of conversations cause relationships to regress, and unfortunately, you'll only have to work harder next time.

One of the reasons that I like a matter-of-fact, task-tone is that it frames the discussion of a problem as a process of working out the basic steps to resolve it. Years of talking to boys about problems has taught me that a utilitarian approach feels more helpful, and less worrisome, than either an authoritarian ("I'll show you who's the boss!") or overly emotional ("sweetheart, we want you to express your feelings") approach.

When boys are in a jam, they are searching for the way out . . . a set of steps that allows them to make amends for a mistake or shortcoming. They respect and listen to those who serve up options without judgment, and without a tone that feels "emasculating."

Explain What He Should Do

Getting yourself stuck in a difficult situation is stressful. For boys, a sense of agency is key to regaining forward momentum, even if this involves having to do things that tangibly demonstrate remorse. For most, emphasizing solutions is a better option than a long worrisome talk at the kitchen table, during which a boy feels worse and worse. Conversations which rehash mistakes often end without any clear sense of next steps. Conversely, it's amazing how powerful our vocal tone can be in providing reassurance, and clarifying a path forward. A task-tone encourages you to speak in shorter sentences and to focus on concrete actions that lead to specific outcomes. Even if you're making significant demands of a boy's energy and time, the net effect is more manageable for him when you identify any clear steps you want him to take.

As a counterpoint, this is not the sort of vocal tone that one uses when discussing a child's feelings about social anxiety, a death, or minor setbacks like losing a game or class election. Those situations require a different disposition, and boys typically respond better to a softer vocal tone, and different kinds of words. Yet even on those occasions, boys benefit from adults who can successfully bring words to complex feelings. Virtually all boys can label basic emotions. For example, they generally know the difference between sadness and anger, excitement and anxiety. More subtle emotions present a greater challenge — and boys who can navigate emotions with words do a better job of coping with personal challenges, and advocating for themselves. Providing words for emotions can make life situations more tangible and workable for boys. (Incidentally, this is one of the great reasons that psychotherapy is effective for people. When we label our feelings with personally comprehensible words, they become more accessible and manageable.)

Emotions that are not filtered through words have an intimidating power for boys. Consequently, boys will avoid, ignore, or make fun of them. Boys, and many men as well, will do whatever is necessary to distance themselves from what eludes their understanding and control. Ambiguity is generally stressful and unpleasant for males.

When you need to address more difficult emotions with boys, it's helpful to use words that unfold emotions. A good example is addressing disappointment. Having done focus groups with a great many boys in different countries and cultures, I've learned that a parent's disappointment can be emotionally devastating. Certainly, we as parents have a right to be disappointed in our sons, but it's somewhat unfair not to explain the genesis of those feelings. It's also helpful to provide a little bit of insight about why you might be using a specific word or phrase to describe a situation or reaction. For example, "I'm disappointed in how you handled the conflict with your brother. He looks up to you for guidance, and you're very capable. I'm not angry, I'm just a little disappointed."

A matter-of-fact, workmanlike approach describes a practical problem that might lead to a tangible course of action. It's effective because boys can sense that the conversation has a purposeful trajectory and an end point. The latter is of immeasurable importance. The notion that there is a conclusion to conversation indicates that there is some point when enough will have been said, and a situation will have been resolved.

This idea may not resonate well with those accustomed to long and complex conversations. Some may be less focused on a specific resolution than the importance of talking itself. Certainly, this is an equally legitimate way of conversing, and many of my therapist colleagues would defend this value. But in my view that way of talking is alien to many, if not most males; it is too ambiguous, and acts as an impediment to future conversation.

Once you have established a task-tone with boys, and they have become accustomed to hearing you use it, it becomes possible to use the tone to leverage greater emotional comprehension. Let's agree that we want to raise boys who are emotionally intelligent, sophisticated, and sensitive to nuance. It's just that we can't get to that place without first establishing a tone of confidence and clarity.

Practicing Your Task-Tone

You may have some concern about your own ability to replicate this tone. Experience suggests this is especially true for many women, who have expressed apprehension about whether the tone I'm suggesting could ever become natural for them. That's a fair question, but not a dead end. What's most important is that you develop a tone that is noticeably different from how you typically communicate. Boys will learn to tune into that difference; they will understand that you're in a different state of mind when the terms of communication have shifted. Also, you can still employ the strategies I'm recommending, including shorter, more succinct sentences, less vague, open-ended questions, and more clarity about what to do next.

The key is to have more than one channel for communicating. Practically speaking, you need at least two, and the less familiar one will probably require some practice. Practice speaking in task-tone while driving alone, or in other situations where you can carefully listen to the sound of your own voice. Few of us ever do this, even when it comes to the voice we use most of the time. Good practice includes experimenting with speaking more slowly, and with pausing after you make an important point. Practice asking forced-choice questions (Do you want to do A, B, or C?), rather than open-ended ones (So, what would you like to do?). I know open-ended seems better and fairer, but for many kids vague choices are a stressful conversation stopper.

The *timbre* of your voice is affected by how much vibration you allow to affect your vocal chords. Timbre can be harmonic, and small differences can make it easier for others to listen, and join with you. When you get pitch and timbre just right, your voice serves as a pleasant auditory focal point — boys will enjoy talking with you because your vocal tone suggests a safe, constructive, mutually respectful relationship.

As you practice a task-tone, concentrate on reducing emotion, suspiciousness, or an attitude of prosecution. It's not that we don't want boys to address emotions in their lives, it's just that we need to be strategic in getting them to that point. Task-tone defuses their apprehension and uncertainty about what is OK to feel.

It's OK for boys to feel whatever they feel, but many a promising conversation has flopped by stating that very point at the beginning! What feels reassuring to you may stir up confusion and anxiety in boys.

Often, we have our most important conversations with boys at moments when we are tense or anxious. At such times, it's human nature to want to explain ourselves. Our anxious mind suggests to us that if only the other person could see things as we do, everything would be better — there would be more consensus and less conflict. However strong that urge may be, *please don't succumb to the temptation to use long, reasoned explanations, believing they will make conversation safe and constructive.* As adults, it's often counterproductive to explain our way through conversations with boys. The content of our words may be logical and clear to us, but ultimately words will fall short. We do a much better job when we focus on controlling nonverbal aspects of communication, like tone and eye contact. These are the keys to establishing comfort and respect. Once you know how to create a comfortable and respectful conversational atmosphere, you can bring up all kinds of content, and it will have a much better chance of registering.

Be a Coach, Not a Boss

Let's take our examination of vocal tone one important step further. Sometimes when people hear me demonstrating task-tone they mistakenly interpret the tone as authoritarian or bossy, because of the lower pitch and my comfort with being directive. (Boys, themselves, rarely make this error.) My intention, however, is to avoid a "boss" or "drill sergeant" persona and instead to speak more like a coach. Bosses and coaches are similar in some ways, but they are also different in even more important ways. For example, a boss and a coach may both have high expectations, but a boss (at least a bad one) can be authoritarian, while a coach is authoritative. It's the difference between a "my way or the highway" attitude, and "Try this my way, I think it will help you. If it doesn't, we'll find something that does." A coach is on your side and wants you to succeed. A "boss" often puts his or her own needs first. Another important difference is how your communication affects your proximity to a boy. Specifically, a boss is more likely to confront, while a coach is more likely to support. A coach is "behind" you, in a supportive position. Don't get me wrong, coaches can certainly be pushy, but they don't stand in judgment of you. A coach's goal is to achieve improved performance and a "win." Coaches are not primarily involved in assigning blame or causing guilt. A good coach quickly puts a mistake in the past, and focuses on the next opportunity for success. A coach wins and loses with the team. The same sort of collaboration at home or in school is of great value — and it all starts with your vocal tone. By using a task-tone you eliminate traces of judgment that can potentially get in the way of communicating important points. I'm not telling you to be unreasonably "soft," or to withhold practical advice. I am strongly encouraging you to make a mental distinction between the voice of a boss vs. that of a coach.

Voice of a . . .

Coach	Boss
High expectations	High expectations
Authoritative	Authoritarian
Stands behind	Confronts
Accepts responsibility for wins and losses	Criticizes and judges

Eye Contact

Eye contact is one of the most misunderstood aspects of communication with boys. Many adults have come to believe that we should always direct boys to make eye contact if they are being spoken to by an adult. Well, there's no doubt that eye contact does convey respect. However, demanding eye contact can make it much more difficult for a boy to listen, formulate questions, or accept advice. Should we demand eye contact as a matter of protocol? I don't believe we should every time, but let me qualify my answer. Overall, I think eye contact is a good idea. We should teach boys that they "listen" with their eyes as well as their ears. Yet there are instances when such an expectation is counterproductive. For example, when boys are feeling awkward, shy, or vulnerable, demanding eye contact can get in the way of establishing safety and trust. If a boy has just made a significant mistake and has been reprimanded, eye contact in the immediate moments following this episode heightens shame and anxiety. There may be a few times when it's appropriate to draw on the power of those emotions, but in many cases eye contact unnecessarily increases a boy's fear and apprehension. While I have encouraged you to be aware that boys will look at your eyes as a way of understanding your disposition, I just as quickly caution you against looking too deeply into their eyes. That sort of gaze intimidates boys, and pushes them away.

Cracking the Boy Code is focused on positive outcomes. I hope that's your purpose in reading it. With that premise in mind, let me suggest that there are two types of people who come to psychotherapy: first are those who want a positive outcome and will do whatever is required to get there as fast as possible. Second are those who want success, but insist on arriving at that outcome on their own terms — whether those terms are realistic or not. The latter group spends a lot more time in psychotherapy because their inflexibility makes it harder to achieve the desired goal. That's the type of situation you get yourself into when you insist that a boy makes eye contact. The reality is that many boys listen better, committing your thoughts and suggestions to long-term memory, when they are not making eye contact.

Strategic application of eye contact is important because it is a primal form of signaling. Looking into the eyes of another person is one of our most instinctual reflexes because it is an immediate and highly productive way of gathering information about another person's state of mind. In fact, eye contact is so efficient and reliable that we learn to use it from an early age. Even children who are too young to understand all the words spoken to them watch the eyes of an adult as a means of gathering information about what that adult is saying, or wants them to do.

For our purposes, it's important to recognize that a person's eyes are a primary means of conveying safety and trust. I learned this many years ago when I began treating boys, and on the first meeting would introduce myself in the waiting room. I noticed how intensely they looked at me, studying my face for any sign of what sort of person I might be. I noticed that I inadvertently disrupted their attention if I studied them back just as closely. It became obvious to me that using the right amount of eye contact would make things go much smoother. It isn't enough just to care about boys, or to be committed to helping them. We should translate those good intentions into visible signals that boys can readily understand as signs of acceptance and calm.

Most boys can sense when someone is working hard to decode them by staring into their eyes. They usually feel that sort of close observation as intrusive. Remember that if a boy has trouble picking up and interpreting other people's visual cues, he is equally uncomfortable when others try to read his own. Although boys are inadvertently sending these signals, it makes them feel uncomfortable to think they are giving information away which others might use to gain a conversational advantage. Generally, boys don't want to be studied. When they do feel studied, they tend to be avoidant. Most measure their words carefully, and respond only as much as they absolutely need to. Many parents tend to sit across from a child, making unrelenting eye contact during a fact-finding, kitchen table conversation. This is one reason why a family's kitchen table is such a perilous place to have an important conversation!

The problem is unfortunately compounded if we happen to hear something unexpected, and react by showing too much shock in our eyes. A startled reaction is often a conversation killer because it suggests "you've done something weird or extreme." A boy between the ages of 10 and 15 is likely to get away from that sort of feedback as fast as he can.

Dos and Don'ts of Eye Contact

Helpful	Unhelpful
During moment of chaos or distraction	When you or the child is upset or angry
Personalizing direction or advice (briefly)	With self-conscious or anxious children
Supportive listening, or to admire an accomplishment	Right after a mistake

Strategy for Difficult Moments

The next time you want to tell a boy what a fine job he's done, make sure to look him in the eye when you tell him. But when you bring up a more sensitive topic, try having the conversation in a setting where the two of you are sitting side by side, both of you looking straight ahead. Can you think of such a setting that occurs routinely? Of course, it is in your car. Driving with a boy is an ideal place to have a conversation about more sensitive matters. Any prospective tension is reduced when both people are looking forward, rather than at one another. For boys, there is also something about the motion of a car that facilitates relaxation and the flow of communication. Even with a younger child who may be required to sit in the back seat, good conversations can be had. There's a practical side to this strategy as well: we spend so much time bringing kids to various activities that it seems ridiculous to waste that time. I've heard many parents say that car time is some of their favorite time with boys. Obviously, if you're careening down the highway at 75 mph, weaving in and out of lanes, a car ride won't work too well as a platform for conversation. But you don't have to be cruising down the perfect country lane either. If you take some driving routes consistently, boys will become increasingly comfortable with great drive-talks. (If you don't drive, a similar result can be accomplished on public transportation if you can find a more private spot.) Mix it up so that the topic isn't all business; school, sports, family, and politics are usually of great interest to boys. Employing a variety of topics reinforces a crucial lesson: fun and seriousness are complementary, and they fit together to shape a more complete life and relationship.

> Begin with a topic that is comfortable for your son, and then transition. If your son is sitting in the front seat, combine your communication with some sort of supportive physical contact. That sort of contact feels reassuring and friendly, and most boys will accept this as a signal of affection or love.

Simplicity, Safety, and Trust

Another person's eyes are decoded primarily in the right hemisphere of the brain. As we saw in earlier chapters, this part of a boy's brain does not always function as effectively as the part that hears words and makes sense of the structural parts of language (left hemisphere). For example, boys often get confused by subtle facial expressions, especially when they do not immediately appear to match a person's words or tone of voice. When two people know each other well, or if you have moved into a deeper conversation, it may be useful to use more complex expressions. However, when you're trying to get a conversation going, work hard to establish trust and safety and use more readily comprehensible facial expressions. It's especially important to use your eyes in a welcoming way.

The most basic way of conveying a welcoming attitude with your eyes is to keep them more open, and to relax the muscles around your eyes and in your forehead. As a rule, when your face is physically relaxed, your expression will match.

It's always a good idea to practice facial expressions in a mirror so that you know what your face looks like when you use your facial muscles in a particular way. It won't take long to make these associations more automatic, but you should, at least once, notice exactly how your face looks when you move your eyes and eyebrows to create different types of smiles. Please don't assume your self-awareness is only important for more active facial expressions. Your "resting face" is equally important. Unfortunately, some people have a way of looking angry or irritated when they're lost in thought. My intention isn't to stress you out. You shouldn't have to be "presenting" your face every moment of the day. Yet I do notice that parents sometimes "look glum" in social situations, and I know kids are receiving that signal, even when it's unintentional.

Remember

- Vocal tone is the most important signal you send about your state of mind, and where a conversation is going.
- *Task-tone* relaxes boys. It is both succinct and respectful, encouraging boys to be less defensive and more responsive.
- Eye contact should be used carefully. At moments of heightened stress or vulnerability, less eye contact is preferable. Many boys listen and hear better when eye contact is reduced.

Points to Consider

- Have you spent any time listening to your own voice, and the range of your vocal tone?
- Do you have a natural task-tone, or do you need to cultivate one?
- Can you be comfortable having a close conversation with less eye contact? Are you remembering to stay away from the kitchen table?

Part II

Deepening the Conversation

Chapter 6

Authenticity — Helping Boys Become Themselves

W HAT IF THERE WERE AN ACCELERATOR that helped boys mature, and become men? Specifically, what if there were a counterpoint to distraction, misbehavior, self-absorption, and poor motivation? There is an answer to these growing pains, lodged deep inside a boy's psychology. The answer is a grasp of one's authentic self. The idea is straightforward enough, but the process must be learned repeatedly by successive generations. This formative path in a boy's life is more important than school grades, athletic skills, and good manners. In acknowledging the infinite importance of authenticity, we shift from thinking about what *we* want from boys toward what is most important for *them*.

There can be no compromise when it comes to authenticity, because without it boys are lost. True, they may still be excellent students and good sons in some respects, but without authenticity they lack a personal compass. Knowing one's authentic self is a tool for sorting out difficult decisions, for sensing what is right. Have you ever met a boy who is so identified with parents that he measures the success of his decisions by whether his parents will agree? That boy is lost. His parents may be extraordinarily wise, but that young person is unprepared to face life's difficulties with the courage it takes to persevere in the face of confusion and adversity. Authenticity contributes mightily to strong convictions and emotional resilience. It is foundational to every significant achievement in a young person's life.

Key Premises

Pondering big concepts like authenticity, it's easy to get caught in abstractions and a misunderstanding of basic assumptions. This is a challenge that comes up in a clinical setting like my office, and which I want to address here. All participants need to be on the same page. Most people are reading this book as a means of getting practical advice. Whatever guidance I can provide about authenticity is based on certain assumptions about childhood and youth, for example how people change and develop. These beliefs are the foundation of my insights, and I think it is important — and fair — that I share them with you.

One of my basic assumptions is that *personhood is fluid and malleable*. If I didn't believe this, it would be pointless to offer advice on how to shape the development of a child. Even though growth as a process is widely acknowledged, many retain a deterministic understanding of human character development. Some consider that genes are the definitive building blocks of personhood, the final determinants of a person's temperament and character. There is certainly good reason to respect the role of genes in shaping personality and behavior, but noting this fact is where discussion about other influences should begin, not end. All people contend with the influence of genes, but that should not lead us to a place of resignation. Instead, we should focus on which aspects of a boy's development can be affected by guidance and experience.

Let me clarify what I mean by personhood being "fluid." First, it doesn't always mean steady, positive momentum. Sometimes that's true, but fluid can just as easily mean a state of chaos or regression. In fact, that sort of upheaval is usually what brings a person or family into my office. The notion of a life in chaos is anxiety-provoking, but think of a milder form of chaos, such as flux, and your perspective might brighten. One of the gifts of youth is a more flexible mind. This is true on both a biological and psychological level. Young people are wired to learn, and many are sponges for knowledge that can lead them toward a life consistent with their needs and ideals. I realize some boys are instead bound by rigid thinking, and repetitive, self-sabotaging behavior. But even those individuals will allow themselves to be positively influenced when they believe others are advocating for their happiness, rather than trying to control them.

The Spell of Self-Absorption

If we can agree that a boy's search for his authentic self requires him to turn inward, we must still acknowledge the distinction between constructive reflection, and a more directionless infatuation characteristic of self-absorption. You've probably seen these episodes as boys stare into the distance, anesthetized by electronics. Circular thinking and fascination with the trivial are major impediments to the insight and experimentation central to an authentic life. *There is a major difference between daydreams and imagining personal objectives.* The reasons for the current epidemic of self-absorption are complex. In my view, it's a mistake to view this social phenomenon as a moral failing, symptomatic of a specific generation. The context in which young people are growing up has contributed to the inertia of self-absorption. For example, there seems to be dysfunctional interaction between brain development and the changing conditions of the world. We have seen a great increase in sources of trivial amusement, and a general "flattening" of life priorities. I'm incredibly optimistic about the coming generation in some ways. For example, they know a lot more about the environment than most members of my generation; they're also more tuned in to how technology can enhance life. At the same time, they waste huge amounts of time, mostly on trivial amusement. I'm concerned that all this lost time will catch up with them.

It is difficult for many young men to see why some things are much more important than other things. The net effect is that they move through life without sensitivity to what is resonant and has enduring value. Arguably, one of the most radical statements we make in our present world is "take your time." Knowing oneself requires time. A key objective in my two decades working with the psychology of boys is to lead them toward being whole people. By this, I mean becoming people with strong self-awareness, as well as the capacity to attend to other people. Herein lies *a key difference between self-absorption and authenticity:* while both mental states involve turning inward, only authenticity puts selfhood in context, helping boys to define themselves in relation to others, and new experiences.

Key Idea: Finding authenticity involves social thinking and experimentation with new activities. The self-absorbed child may never leave his head.

Let's face it, we can't discuss the problem of self-absorption without noting the powerful role of electronica. This includes games, phones, and all related devices. The adverse effects of electronica have their roots in the flickering lights and fragmented audio of television. By now, the dulling of human minds through electronic means is old news. How electronica shapes the psychology of boys, however, is not clearly understood. If screen culture diminishes the neurology of boys, and especially their attention, what is the effect of a life built around the pursuit of trivial amusement? *One of electronica's subliminal messages is that you expect and then react. This patterning has lessened the human capacity to create, and weakened our will to bring things into being.* The net result is *spectator culture.* True, the spectacles may be sensational: who can doubt the power of video graphics and sound to light up a person's sensorium? But who, also, can't see that boys grow up in an endless hallway of images with dubious moral messages? Each image they encounter clamors for attention and a response, and yet the sheer abundance of images suggests that none are fully real, or worth contemplating. Still, stimulation is a thirst that is never quenched — that's what makes electronics addictive. Depending on your perspective, we are blessed or cursed with systems like Xbox where games becomes more and more realistic, but never truly become life itself.

I believe this context can lead to a kind of personal paralysis for many boys. They struggle to make commitments, because making a commitment means to declare your allegiance to something. Where is allegiance to be placed in this electronic hallway of images? How are boys to know what is authentic, and what is disposable? I don't believe that the average boy has any real sense about what is real and what is "costume" in his life. Instead, I believe their psychology prompts them to try on various roles, but then immediately doubt that role because of a steady stream of persuasive alternatives.

The overriding promise of many games is a position of dominance. Being dominant has become an expectation for many boys, amplifying self-absorption and undermining empathy. Many in the current generation anticipate greatness without sacrifice, or any meaningful physical connection to the world. Even in the age of electronica, this sort of expectation is unnatural — nowhere to be found outside of the realm of e-battles. Real combat veterans have much to teach boys about the gap between fantasy and actual human battle. Veterans have paid a high price for that authentic knowledge.

Let's Be *Real*

In talking about authenticity, it is not my intention to propel an abstract idea which can't be practically realized. The authenticity we should instill in boys is as much about a way of loving, as it is about finding oneself. We, as parents, need to come to grips with this idea. If we are focused only on leveraging an outcome, we will miss the chance to help boys grasp the gravity and relevance of their day-to-day lives. There is transcendence in boys' lives, but it is a *pragmatic transcendence* in which one's purpose and role are defined by doing something tangible. This could be academics or sports, but might as easily be some type of work. Tangible achievement is the core path of strength and honor. *Boys need to do good work in an honorable way.*

If you're thinking this is a puritanical, overly strict approach, I ask you to reconsider. We need to work together to save boys from the despair of a life without soul or direction.

The cultivation of authenticity begins early in life, before age ten for most boys. By six or seven, most are ready to explore activities and interests that will, over time, define their authentic selves. This process unfolds slowly, incrementally increasing a boy's sense of purpose and motivation. As adults, there are steps we can take to enable constructive exploration, but it's not as simple as signing someone up for an authenticity class. The precise way in which authenticity becomes rooted is to some extent a human mystery. The road travelled is necessarily unique for each person. Some of us will have a hard time encouraging authenticity because it has been neglected in our own lives; it feels too painful and frustrating to foster something that remains unfinished for ourselves. But don't look away from this important task. You can foster your own authenticity, as you encourage and help build it for your son. By doing so, your intentions will be more credible and powerful.

The foremost challenge in talking to boys about authenticity is the tendency for key words to become vague or misunderstood. So, what does authenticity mean? For our purposes, it means *those aspects of a person's selfhood which are essential to his life story and personal coherence.* We should include key experiences, skills, interests, and perspectives which make someone a whole and distinct person. These attributes lead to *personal coherence*, because they comprise the underlying logic that drives a person's thoughts and actions. This, of course, doesn't include everything that's important to a person. You might like lasagna, but that doesn't mean lasagna is fundamental to your authentic self (unless perhaps you are a chef, and lasagna is your signature dish).

On the other hand, you might like to compete in triathlons, and although you have never won an event and make no money from these competitions, you feel strongly that competing in triathlons expresses an essential aspect of who you are. In some ways, it is *what you stand for.* Triathlons could be so central to your authentic self that if you had to stop competing in them, you would feel as though you were a different person. By extension, if someone doesn't know you are a triathlete, they won't know something very important about who you are. Until you began competing in triathlons, you might have not known something *essential* about yourself.

When we ask someone to explore their authenticity, we are asking that they think about their personal truth. This truth comes from

Remember: Even boys who have not discovered a passion sense the value of having one. By adolescence, self-consciousness and worry are increased when boys lack a clear passion — and they don't trust those who give them false assurances that it's unnecessary or premature to have any direction.

important experiences and teachings that feel right and essential to a person. When this is felt about a specific activity, it's more than an arbitrary choice; it feels like something you must do, perhaps something you were born to do.

In the Western world, we are often taught that unbridled passion is a sign of exceptionality and a harbinger of personal happiness. Yet the discovery of authentic passion rarely comes easily for boys. Sometimes they get physically tired or irritable with having to think about the issue. That's what's behind the groan we hear when we ask them to do something other than electronics with free time. "Like what?" they think.

I know from experience that when the topic of authenticity gets brought up for boys, most start thinking about personality traits. This is a natural reflex, but it also obstructs the task of looking deeper. True, someone's personality will certainly influence the kinds of activities that attract him, but authenticity is more than the sum of personality traits. For example, a person may be shy or gregarious, cautious or risk-taking, humorous or serious. Yet no matter how well we examine these polarities, they will not give us a meaningful picture of that person's authentic self. For one, personality traits don't convey beliefs and convictions. And they don't tell us where a person belongs in the world. Consider that shy and outgoing people are found in all types of endeavors, holding a variety of convictions.

How a person thinks about himself may not be visible on the surface. As an example, a person might feel much more social than his behavior suggests. We can't really know a person's priorities without communicating. However most us, including me, make those judgments about

When we are trying to truly understand another person, we inquire with a spirit of discovery rather than interrogation. Be open to what emerges in conversation. Be exceptionally patient. Seek to understand, but accept that boys rarely produce insightful answers on demand. When the communication block gets too big to ignore, empathize with the difficulty of talking about oneself.

others, reflexively, all the time. Along these lines, *it's important not to mistake confusion or limited communication for a lack of complexity.*

For each person, there are moments where personal truth and authenticity are revealed. I often encounter these moments in meetings with boys and families when there is an impasse of understanding. The child's intentions may seem baffling. I hear "why do you want to give up soccer?" or "how come you're defending him?" Such moments cause anxiety, and there is a rush to resolve them by attaching an interpretation before enough is known about a person, or the situation. We have all been on the receiving end of this impulse at one time or another. Like so many boys, we may have tried to fortify ourselves with silence.

Doing Is More Useful than Thinking

For most boys, elements of authenticity are found more readily by doing, than by reflecting or feeling. In my experience, boys can grasp the basic idea of doing something as a way of discovering authenticity. Later there are moments when he must visualize himself in a situation, being and feeling authentic. This requires a little help, and it's appropriate for you, or someone else, to offer some possibilities for consideration. It's OK to be leading in your questions, and a good way to make progress is with "forced choice" questions: "Well if you had a choice, would you rather try website building or cooking? Helping at your mom's office, or being an assistant coach? Writing a play, or having backyard chickens?" Boys like to imagine versions of themselves in different roles. Sometimes, this mental experimentation works. People aren't always thunderstruck by insight. It might be easier to spot what is true and authentic with choices that allow for comparison.

The next hurdle is getting over the tendency to imagine options that are static: something like still pictures of himself dressed in the "uniform" of various activities or occupations. There's not much useful information to be gained from these images. Static images lead to thoughts like, "and now what?" If we're coaching boys to visualize themselves in different roles, we ought to help them unfold those single images into mental video clips.

Many times, the images that we associate with various activities or purposes are clichés; they stem from popular media, or other sources where important elements of identity are ignored. If I suspect a boy feels a great sense of belonging among boatbuilders, I would prefer he watch a video of a boat being built, rather than admire a photo of a well-equipped boatbuilding workshop. The photo might be compelling, but it does not afford the feeling of immersion and connection gained from watching the key activity being done.

If we think of authenticity as a specific trait to be discovered, we are led astray. That sort of thinking reflects a tendency to believe there is a "specialness" that lives in each child that needs to be found for him to be happy. This distortion leads us away from the serious work of self-discovery, but toward narcissism and self-absorption. That misdirection is an enormous hurdle for boys, many of whom are already drawn toward self-absorption via games with little social relevance.

Self-absorption is a young man's defense against diminishment. Conversely, a rush to "inflate" a boy with a sense of specialness through excessive flattery, or adult projections, is generally not a road to anything good. It's merely a compensatory strategy for a child feeling small, insignificant, and powerless. Or in some unfortunate cases, a parent can feel as though the boy's actions are not sufficiently grand to reflect family expectations.

> Authenticity is shaped, more than it is found. Experimentation and participation are indispensable paths to knowing oneself. Authenticity cannot be found through words alone. Doing is essential.

For various reasons, like parental expectation, sibling rivalry, and worry about the future, boys can become so eager for an authentic passion that they prematurely settle on an identity. This is especially true for boys who are highly identified with parents, and who are anxious to please others. In such cases, it's not easy to get the experience one needs to feel more confidently authentic. The relevance of authenticity is vaguely felt by many, but there is a serious lack of opportunity and qualified guidance for this search.

In my clinical work, I sometimes meet families for whom these ideas resonate. I'm deeply thankful to know such people, although simply

Given the urgency associated with imperatives like school grades, it's easy to see how authenticity might be relegated to a feel-good, complementary activity one pursues when one has free time. This is a recipe for unhappiness, and a primary reason for the current worldwide epidemic of restlessness and disconnection among boys and young men. Growth, confidence, and strength cannot happen without challenge.

being enthusiastic about authenticity doesn't guarantee the best sequence of actions. Discussion of authenticity and what it means should be a primary focus of psychotherapy with boys. In my view, there are few kids who do not benefit from this type of discussion, although that doesn't mean the conversation must be so doggedly persistent that boys shut down from stress and boredom. It works best to mix the topic in with more causal inquiry and connection.

Many of the skills I shared in Part I explain how to set the table for conversation. Please note: you can't effectively get to a conversation about authenticity until you've developed some skill with vocal tone, eye contact, and nonverbal relating. Communication brings authenticity into existence. Boys need words to describe their attitudes and insights. Having words to describe what you feel and think makes it more possible to share those ideas with others. Being oriented to the language of self-expression is itself an essential beginning. Getting comfortable with language helps boys with basic terms and distinctions: the difference between being *original* and *authentic*, between a *goal* and an *ideal*, and between *self-expressive* and *self-absorbed*.

Life Narrative

An important reason why we want to get boys going in searching out strengths, interests, and related experiences is that this information helps to frame a personal narrative. By this I mean someone's life story. I make a special point of including strengths in the mix because feeling competent is so central to most boys' sense of comfort and belonging. Still, there is a bigger payoff: having even a peripheral awareness of one's story makes actions more productive, and related to one's purpose. With this spirit there is both a greater willingness to disagree for the sake of defending one's values and purpose, and a greater capacity to understand subjective differences between people.

Accordingly, higher levels of authenticity are associated with a greater willingness to coexist with those whose lives follow a different course. That means feeling unthreatened by those holding different values, whose actions are organized according to different hierarchies. It also stands to reason that higher levels of authenticity are associated with greater perseverance. Conviction grows the more we live an authentic life. *Perseverance is stronger when a boy is propelled by his own values and interests, rather than those that are imposed upon him.*

Next Steps

Readers may agree with the value I'm assigning to authenticity, but still wonder about its *practical applications.* For example, is authenticity merely a sign that a boy's life has greater meaning? How exactly is that practically useful? Where will greater authenticity take a young person? In terms of psychological growth, it certainly seems better to have a high level of self-awareness, but how does this awareness translate into a better life?

Note that for some, "better life" is code for good job and higher earnings. And in fact, authenticity will result in those outcomes for some people. Years ago, I taught a workshop in Harvard University's Career Discovery program — a summer program for students interested in careers in architecture and design. The students enrolled were bright and talented; many were backed by considerable family resources. Practically speaking, they had lots of options, but like most students they were in pursuit of more than a paycheck; they wanted to be happy — I mean really, really happy with their work.

These students had the courage to struggle with that decision, to spend time trying to do technically difficult things which might point them in the right direction. Over the course of working with these students, I developed an exercise that required them to interview people that they knew from different areas of their lives, about how others perceive their talents. Students were encouraged to be open to whatever might emerge during interviews. This activity reinforces how important it is to know what one is good at doing. With such knowledge in hand, a person can better choose paths that maximize success.

Here are some examples of how authenticity can be of practical value. These are real kids and stories drawn from my clinical practice. There is no one, perfect magical fix for every young person. I want to highlight the power of individual experiences — especially those that involve choice, action, and an observable result:

- Terence is a 17-year-old boy who has never done well in school, and who has seen multiple therapists for help with ADHD. He is an avid hiker, often venturing into canyons with his father for multi-day hikes. Twice they have gotten lost, and Terence has gotten them out of a potentially dangerous situation both times. His father has expressed abundant gratitude, and Terence realized that something formative took root in him during those moments of urgency in desert canyons. His perception of himself shifted. He felt a rush of adrenaline, and a strong sense of calm at the same time. His thinking was clear, and he exuded the confidence needed at that critical time. This way of being was surprisingly comfortable for Terence, and emerged as an important personal distinction — a counterpoint to chronic school struggles — and a viable path forward. He is currently the youngest harbormaster to ever serve his hometown in northern New England.

- Several years ago, Dwayne was a sixth-grade student who showed little interest in anything other than YouTube videos. His parents were aggravated about his lack of motivation, preoccupation with games, and what they termed "negative" music. Dwayne was content to sit silently, and listen to their concerns. He never got angry, just shrugged his shoulders and mumbled, "I don't know." One day his uncle called to ask if Dwayne could help with one of his side businesses, selling vintage athletic shoes online. The thought of the work was less than inspiring, but Dwayne agreed because he would be making money, and because he likes his uncle. Several weeks into the work it was apparent that Dwayne was a natural. He proved to be an expert researcher regarding the value of shoes, and he took great interest in the system his uncle used to determine markup and selling strategies. Dwayne's grades in school got marginally better, but the big payoff has been the obvious increase in his happiness. Dwayne has spent far less time moping around the house, and has complained less about being asked to do things. These days he is more likely to complain, "I hate wasting time. I could be building up the business, and making money."

• Marc loves to perform. It doesn't seem to matter what type of performance, Marc loves being on stage, and in front of people. His parents observed this for several years, but assumed that it was a precocious, youthful interest that would eventually pass. When Marc turned 14, it looked like a love of performing was going to stick. The family considered how to respond to Marc's interest, given available time and resources. In Marc's school district, all children must participate in extracurricular sports, but theater is relatively scarce, and somewhat devalued as an activity for teens. The best option seemed to be a charter school that was a more inconvenient drive for Marc's parents. After some family deliberation, Marc's father had a meeting with the charter school, describing his son's interests and difficulties connecting with activities at his current school. Hearing about options, and seeing the theater at the charter school, it was clear that Marc would benefit from being in a different school. The theater was mostly outfitted with old equipment, but Marc's father could sense the seriousness of intent when he walked around backstage. The family made a major decision to enroll Marc in the charter school so that he would have more authorship over the direction of his education. Marc went from being a frustrated spectator to feeling the kind of identification with school which kids long for.

Make Authenticity an Intention

In boys' lives, the search for authenticity establishes a "form" for living. This means staying true to yourself and working hard to sense what feels right and true. An important element of this intention is trying new activities. The goal is to close the gap between ideals and the actual circumstances that make up a person's life. Wouldn't it be better if we all lived lives that better matched our ideals? I know many of us are afraid to even imagine that possibility. We fear we may be disappointed, or we feel ashamed to want something more than what we have. I don't doubt that every life involves compromise, but "settling" shouldn't be the foundation of growing up, even though it is for many. Most young people need steady encouragement and constructive, non-directive involvement. Artful parenting always strikes a balance between pointing the way, and getting out of the way. If we try to micromanage a boy's actions, we smother his spirit with so much concern that irritation or anxiety are likely results.

Strength and honor is about building a powerful foundation of words and thinking skills. We might hope that talking and self-reflection get easier as boys get older, but there's no guarantee. So often, boys resist conversation about their deeper meaning and purpose. They do this because it is tedious and hard work, or because they feel self-conscious about having inadequate answers. This sort of resistance is commonly found in American households, and might sound something like this:

Father: So, are you happy to have finished the school year?

Son: I don't know, I guess so.

Father: Well, are you looking forward to summer?

Son: I guess.

Father: What are you most looking forward to?

Son: I don't know.

Father: There must be something? What do you want to do this summer?

Son: I have no idea. Nothing, I guess.

Father: I have a few thoughts about things you might want to do.

Son: Not interested.

Father: Not interested? You don't even know what they are!

Son: Sorry, I'm just not interested.

Father: Not interested in what?

Son: Anything.

Father: You're uninterested in everything. How is that possible?

Son: I'm sick of talking about this.

Such conversations are mutually frustrating; I recommend psychotherapy as an alternate place to explore self-knowledge and authenticity. Therapy offers the advantage of open-minded conversation about what is in a person's best interest, without any pressure to please someone else. For young people, *dialogue in a safe space* creates the environment in which a boy can think through his own assumptions. Among other things, this dialogue must let go of rigid ideas about who a boy is, or how he might find success. If your relationship with your son is hampered by too many inflexible beliefs, it will be more difficult for him to find his authentic self. The task will be mixed up with either wanting to please you, or perhaps wanting to rebel against you. In either case that lost emotional energy is a distraction from the primary task at hand.

The Investment Approach

It's crucial to have your child move toward *individual decision-making* and *goal-directed actions*, and away from the *investment approach*. The investment approach to youth can be found everywhere; it's exemplified by the high school student who participates in lots of extracurricular activities to optimize his chances of admission to a better university. On the surface, maybe not such a bad idea. But the investment approach is also expressed by intrusive parenting, where every decision affecting education and development is focused on a mythic outcome (riches, status, prestige) to be realized in adulthood. An investment approach to life *devalues the importance of life in the present.* It deprives young people of an opportunity to learn how to be themselves at a time when inclinations and new experiences can help shape their personhood.

Although boys may be capable exploring their authentic selves at a young age, many will not come to this search until some years later, and indeed most may be young men before they understand the need to dig deeper.

It can be difficult to embrace your individuality in the "noise" of daily life. Authenticity sometimes needs a constructive period of separateness and partial detachment. This is an opportunity to sort out personal priorities apart from the persistent distractions and influences of popular culture and people. Wilderness is ideal for this process wherever it can be accessed. There are times when social connections can block the possibility of self-examination.

Boys need to encounter their individual selves in a psychological space not preoccupied with neurotic distractions about how they are like or different from peers. Social media may be widely enjoyed by boys, but it doesn't lead any individual toward authenticity. There is no possibility of becoming your own person if you are entirely fixated on others, or how others perceive you.

It is especially important to do the foundational work of authenticity before attaching to the idea of accomplishments. Some accomplishments may be critical benchmarks in the process, *but meaningful accomplishments reflect ideals that must come from the child, and not his parents, teachers, or mentors.* This is difficult and disciplined work. There are many boys who find such challenges to be stressful and confusing. A strong character is needed to search for truth without being distracted, or looking away because you don't like what you see. This is when encouragement and belief, especially from parents, is critical. Use task-tone to talk about these important issues in a matter-of-fact way. Make these conversations a normal part of family life.

Remember

- Electronica undermines the development of authenticity. Boys don't begin figuring out who they are until they escape the barrage of representations and distractions that occupy their lives.
- Authenticity means that which is essential to a person's life story and personal coherence. These insights and experiences are the glue that hold boys together at critical forks in the road.
- Cultivating authenticity has practical value. It instills confidence, direction, and effort. It is a buffer against anxiety and depression.

Points to Consider

- Do you have terms for discussing authenticity with boys?
- Have you resolved how to answer relevant questions about your own life?
- Are you open-minded about how authenticity might emerge?
- Will you be OK with interests or passions that are markedly different from your own?

Chapter 7

Boys and Work

W E'VE BEEN LOOKING AT THE IMPORTANCE of finding one's authentic self, which can seem like an entirely mental task. The message that most boys get, intentionally or unintentionally, is that they're supposed to think their way through figuring out who they are. That's the result of being asked lots of reflective questions, for which most have few answers. Almost none can solve the problem by thought alone. I don't even recommend trying! The best approach is to literally work through this challenge.

Let me boldly go one step further: *the primary missing ingredient in the lives of people under age 25, the opportunity that separates them from a sense of personal accomplishment, maturity, and resilience, is **purposeful work**.* It's work that propels confidence, esteem, and grit. This idea can be a hard sell in a culture that craves leisure and amusement. Even if you agree with me about the value of work, can you see the problem? Boys live in a spectator world, and they resist being pulled out of that passive, unproductive reality. For many, life is a never-ending loop of games. Why are these distractions so powerful? It's easier to be a spectator. It involves less physical energy, and less social thinking. *Yet purposeful work is an unrecognized key to a life of direction and fulfillment.* Satisfaction and pride flow out of work. Wisdom and experience teach us this truth, and it is imperative for families and schools to orient young people to this idea.

Given the enormous role that work plays in life, it's striking that there is so little dialogue with boys about the transformative power of work. Purposeful work is an activity that calls someone to do something which can be both meaningful and personally transformative. It may be a given task that is difficult to learn, but that's OK because overcoming difficulty makes the task more significant, and more relevant to knowing yourself.

If it seems unusual to be thinking of boys as *workers,* please be open-minded. Involvement in work improves the capacity for effort and attention — which are major hopes for the current generation of parents.

There are no specific restrictions on what type of work this might be, nor should there be any bias toward work that is inherently mental or physical. Working outdoors, in an office, alone or among others, are all equally eligible choices. Context and age have a lot to do with determining what purposeful work might be. Here are just a few examples:

6–8 year-olds
- Helping to stamp envelopes, making sure the alignment and adhesion are correct.
- Picking up toys, and making decisions about where and how to store them.
- Helping to pack a lunchbox, and helping to shop for needed ingredients.
- Creating and leading a game for a younger sibling.

9–11 year-olds
- Helping with hand-tool repairs around the home.
- Helping to paint a room.
- Helping plan a party for a sibling.
- Taking care of a family pet.

12–14 year-olds
- Working on a family farm, or at a community garden.
- Volunteering at a local museum or library.
- Learning the basics of architectural drawing; working on the redesign of school spaces.

- Creating a Minecraft server that provides monetized services to other players.
- Shoveling snow for neighbors.

15 year-olds and beyond

- Apprenticing to a craftsperson.
- Starting a small business (fishing guide for younger kids, pet care)
- Work at a local business involving a new skill.
- Writing a play for a summer theater camp.
- Developing expertise in buying and selling collectibles.

Defining Purposeful Work

Purposeful work is practical. It invites belief in a boy's right and responsibility to script his own life — to pursue work that is ideal because it is related to one's ideas about what is important to do. Looking at the examples I've provided, you might not think of them as exalted, life-changing opportunities. That's OK. We should remember that *it is the tone and attitude we bring to assigning and collaborating on tasks that wins the hearts and minds of boys.* That connection is critical, so let me break it down a bit more. When a person does work that in some way elevates their status, that work is psychologically reinforcing. It is very satisfying to do that type of inherently social task. It is social because it is done for, or with regard for, others.

Along those lines, I strongly recommend using personal language when asking boys to engage. For example, "Would you help me set up Mom's computer?" or "I'd really appreciate your ideas on how to reorganize the garage" or "I know it's a lot to ask right now, but your participation makes all the difference." This type of language is good emotional intelligence. It reflects appreciation that it is easier for boys to join with an effort in which they feel valued. Of course, encouragement doesn't mean that task will not be difficult, tiring, or complex. It's just that those hurdles are more easily overcome when the emotional atmosphere is positive.

Pursuing purposeful work is not the same as fantasizing about having a dream job. *The notion of a so-called dream job disempowers almost everyone because it suggests good and satisfying work is as improbable and as unreal as a dream.* What is often meant by a "dream job" is an easy, cushy job, with few expectations and high pay. Boys who fixate on such fantasies have lost or never known the pleasure of more purposeful work. Among other things, it is work that contributes to something of tangible, visible benefit, and which serves relevant human needs. The type of work I am endorsing is not exclusive to those with advanced degrees, or to the most gifted members of society. It is accessible to everyone willing to discover and shape their own industry. This is the productive path to figuring out who you are, and where you fit into the world.

If the idea and urgency of purposeful work strikes you as odd or confusing, then I'm concerned about your own history of work. The harsh reality is that many, if not most of us, have had insufficient opportunity to do purposeful work. It's not surprising if we feel reflexively opposed to the effort and time work requires. Among younger people especially, work may stand directly opposite to pleasure: an obligation, and intrusion into personal space. Boys often learn to distract themselves while working as a means of decreasing their annoyance with having to do things that feel alien to who they imagine themselves to be. A big part of the problem is that so many boys are doing work that lacks a significant opportunity to learn and problem-solve. Let's face reality. It's hard to take ownership of tasks that don't seem to reflect positively on your abilities. Too few truly interesting and challenging opportunities are offered to young people. It's no wonder so many are disillusioned by the work that's offered to them.

This challenge was a major part of my own youth. I began working at my first "real jobs" when I was 14. Having grown up in a working-class family, I was eager to have my own money, and I knew a couple of boys who were dishwashers at a local restaurant. I got my working papers signed by my parents, and got a job as a dishwasher. It was brutal. Much more washing of large pots and pans than dishes. I was among the last to leave the kitchen at night, my clothes soaked and filthy. I needed a better job, and after a few months found one at the local mall. I was still washing dishes, but this restaurant had a big automatic conveyor dishwasher. The only problem was that the manager would make me do irritating tasks like go outside and start his car for him on a cold winter night. That's rough in January, in New England. Then, when I was 15, I got a job at the local bicycle shop. The job provided an important moment of reckoning in my life, although I didn't appreciate being on the sales floor. In my view, it was much cooler to be a mechanic than a salesperson. The way the mechanics talked seemed more masculine (flip and irreverent). I kept asking to do that type of work, even as I was learning to interact with customers and sell bikes. One day, to my total amazement, I managed to sell a Schwinn Paramount for $1000 (a huge amount of money for a bicycle in 1977)! The feeling was overwhelming, and I was glad the owner had stuck to his conviction that I belonged on the sales floor rather than the repair shop. This success gave me pride, and helped me to understand the social complexity of helping a person make a purchase. I had learned about the rigors of work as a dishwasher, but I didn't find myself in work until I sold bicycles. By adolescence, boys are physically and mentally ready to engage serious, consequential exploration of their interests and abilities.

In the 1880s, before they solved the problem of flight, Wilbur and Orville Wright started a newspaper (*West Side News*) in their hometown of Dayton, Ohio. Beyond writing their own articles, they occasionally reprinted articles from other publications. Their selections often reflected their own core values and beliefs, many of which had been instilled in their own childhoods. One such article was called "Encourage your Boy," which originally appeared in *Architect and Building News*. The advice endorsed by the Wright brothers is succinct:

> "Too many men make their boys feel that they are of little or no account while they are boys."

> "Do not wait for the boy to grow up before you begin to treat him as an equal."

> "If a boy finds he can make a few articles with his hands, it tends to make him rely on himself. And the planning that is necessary for the execution of the work is a discipline and education of great value to him."[1]

Clearly, the world has changed since the era in which these thoughts were written, but the basic truth is still relevant. *We promote maturity, self-reliance, and self-knowledge by giving boys real opportunities to contribute through various types of work.* Our biggest challenge may be a shrinking number of work options for boys. *In a digital world, there are less opportunities to contribute physically in the world.*

Watching, and Still More Watching

Beyond an absence of interesting, purposeful options, boys resist work because it is a departure from life as a spectator. Hanging out as a spectator has less to do with an epidemic of laziness, than it does with the hypnotic fascination so many of us have with nonstop watching. As we all know, a huge proportion of information is accessed through screens of various types, and this seems to hold true regardless of education, socioeconomic status, gender, or age. Our preference for observing rather than doing, or to believe we *are* doing when we are actually watching, has become so reflexive that it may defy detection. For example, when a habit becomes so commonplace that it feels natural, what is there to detect? Our inclination to watch is also a bigger issue than spending hours each day looking at screens. Specifically, our obsession with visual stimulation is testament to how much we live inside our heads. A mind focused on its next stimulatory "fix" moves in a circular manner, accomplishing little. A never-ending loop of images, sounds, and notifications is mentally captivating. It also makes life outside of such captivity seem dull, slow, and irrelevant.

Work *and* Play

The difficulty of suggesting that work is good for young people is partly due to the zealous defense of play that now dominates discussions of childhood. Many defenders of early childhood play argue that childhood should be free of responsibility, and that children are over-pressured. Naturally, resistance to any proposal for how children might be more meaningfully productive, or that *productivity is fundamental to their sense of inclusion,* can follow. In my view, the attempt to keep childhood free of too much pressure has had the right target, but the wrong response. No sane person wants children to be fixated on being promoted to the perfect primary school. I am a strong believer in the cognitive and emotional advantages of constructive play, particularly for younger children.

It seems important, however, to clarify the difference between how a child is encouraged to relate to play, and how that same child might be guided toward relating to work. Where play provides an opportunity for the dramatic projection of fantasies and conflicts, work is accountable to human, animal, and environmental needs. By extension, it is inherently social, even when it is done alone. Work demands that creativity and selfhood be used to accomplish something that is relevant beyond one individual's immediate needs and wants. The natural role-play of young children is purposeful when it involves pretending to be a firefighter, doctor, astronaut, or superhero. It is when pretending to "be" something transitions to a screen-based activity that "play" diminishes the child's authorship. In electronic play the script is defined by others, and the "doing" occurs only on a screen.

Play occupies life before work does. In some ways, it is a primer for personal industry. Early childhood play almost always has a purpose — a task to be accomplished. In some cases, the spirit of work and play are barely distinguishable. A good example of the borderland between play and work is children's literature, which focuses on characters who are agents of positive action, and who fulfill the immediate needs of a community. As cleverly observed by writer Alain de Botton, children gravitate toward characters who are "shopkeepers, builders, cooks or farmers — *people whose labor can easily be linked to the visible betterment of human life* [my emphasis]."[2]

Children's books help illuminate the conversion of playfulness into industry that can be observed and practically measured. As the prospective roles of adulthood come into sharper focus, the ideals of young people often hover over work that is creative, expressive, and which results in a *visible* and *admirable outcome*. Young people usually hope for jobs that will win them admiration. *That sort of emotional reward is a primary motivation for working in the first place.* This helps to explain why so few fantasize about being data analysts, managers, or vice presidents, relative to the possibility of fame. Many falsely believe that we do young people a service when we advise them that work is necessary drudgery to be done primarily for money. That sort of vibe can set a dark and ominous cloud over a young person's life. A much better approach is to orient boys to work as a process of self-discovery, experimentation, and purpose.

Boys Need Purposeful Options

People of all ages, and young people more than others, are in immediate and desperate need of education about work and vocation. Helping boys as young as six or seven to discover purpose and accomplishment through work is especially critical. Opportunity is abundant if adults take the time to frame simple activities as serious, and if we are inventive in balancing responsibility with independence. Younger boys are thrilled to be given tasks that require them to make decisions, and to exercise good judgment. When work is purposeful, it helps younger people to join with its momentum, identify with its outcome, and to accept the difficulties involved. Learning what's required in the process makes work transcendent. By *transcendent*, I mean *work that shapes a person's way of thinking about himself.* If a task does not hold that possibility, it is probably better understood as labor than work.

Work vs. Chores

Please don't misunderstand me. We all do chores to make our lives and households run. It's part of life, and boys should play their role. But labor and chores don't offer the same opportunity which work offers: helping to define yourself. I know many of us are used to thinking of work as a tiresome nuisance, but purposeful work is more creative, and involves a learning curve that leads to greater self-confidence. The potential for work to be personally meaningful increases when the chosen work draws upon one's abilities and interests. This is not an impossibility, even for younger kids. In my practice, I often spend time on this challenge, and I see good examples all around me. I have a 14-year-old neighbor who finds it intensely purposeful to fell trees with a chainsaw, and another who is on her way to a pet-care enterprise. These are "dream" jobs of people finding personal significance through work. These work tasks require distinct forms of practical intelligence. They also require decision-making, time and money management, and communication with others.

Not every purposeful job will pay wages or a salary. Sometimes the most important reward is how work changes the way a boy feels about himself.

Almost every successful person can recall transformational work experiences — and can explain how those activities were influential. I appreciate that it can be hard to think of what this sort of work might be for the boy you know. I don't like to limit anyone's imagination, but in the interest of being useful, I've included an appendix of Fifty Ideas for Purposeful Work. This should give you a broad and strong starting point to think about how to help your own son.

Character

There are some who might suggest that the purpose of work in young people's lives is to build character. You're not likely to have much luck selling that idea to young people. Almost as soon as boys get a whiff of that agenda, their interest in work diminishes. Basically, the work ceases to be animated by a sense of purpose, and is instead propped up by moral obligation. Don't most of us feel the same about our own work? I think most people want to be interested in our work. *There is no joy quite like the feeling of being paid to do something that fulfills you.* Although we can hope that character is the outcome of good work, making character development the objective of work for boys undermines its attractive resonance. Too much focus on character makes work the means to an end, rather than something that has inherent value.

When work is done cooperatively with other people, there is almost always an expectation of good conduct, even if that expectation is unspoken. Problems emerge primarily in cases where good conduct means burying personal needs or interests. These work circumstances are commonly found in large corporations or in retail businesses that require specific, scripted or coerced conduct. Of course, such constraints are going to diminish an individual's sense of self. If we want young people to really get into work, we will need to develop workplaces that encourage (rather than oppress) initiative and self-expression. Happily, many corporations are making efforts in this direction. Sadly, they are the exception and not the rule.

Education

One of the primary reasons communities have traditionally accepted responsibility for teaching the young how to work is a common appreciation of how working fosters maturity. Giving up on this responsibility achieves exactly the opposite result. By not teaching boys how to work, we effectively stunt maturity. I know many of us want boys to have jobs, but few of us are involved in teaching young people interesting new things, endowing them with skills, or giving them a chance to meaningfully contribute to community life. Instead, all emphasis is placed on school performance. In my view, *school needs to be infused and driven by the spirit of vocation* — being called to accomplish significant things. Isn't achievement in the wider world a primary value of being educated? Sitting still in classrooms no longer has the relevance it once may have had. It's just not logical to carve a life from a learning environment which is decidedly "hands-off."

Philosopher turned mechanic Matthew Crawford, writes in *Shop Class as Soulcraft*, "[A man] can simply point: the building stands, the car now runs, the lights are on. Boasting is what a boy does, because he has no real effect on the world."[3]

Crawford advocates hands-on learning, with which I strongly agree. In addition, there can be a critical problem of distance (time) between classroom learning and outcome. It simply takes too long to get an opportunity to apply what has been learned in school.

The preparation of young people goes on for many more years than most can tolerate. Why should one have to be in their mid-twenties before having a viable opportunity to gain and demonstrate some form of socially relevant competence — to actively participate in making the world?

Traditionally, apprenticeships began in one's teen years or early twenties. By that time boys are certainly ready to shift from spectator to doer. According to my own research with boys, school also suffers from an absence of real-time urgency and necessity — a void that makes life artificially dull.[4] In a perfect world, schools would play a bigger role in making purposeful work a part of every student's life.

Some schools loathe the idea that their role is to provide preparatory jobs programs, because that seems to undermine the nobility of education. It's an understandable defense against the historic and growing commercialization of education as "merely" preparation of workers. Emphasizing technical trades is one way to help students to discover purposeful work. Yet study of the humanities is essential to building the self-awareness required to know what type of work is good and purposeful for oneself. Yet when study holds the spirit of vocation at a distance, education withholds a principal source of meaning from students. The spirit of vocation lives when we talk about work while students are still in school, and have a chance to relate the abstractions of curriculum to life beyond school.

Boys need to make significant decisions about where to allocate their own time and effort. This is one important aspect of maturity. Given certain conditions, it may be possible to raise or educate a boy who is happily compliant with adult directives, but how will those reflexes serve him later on? *The time to begin practicing how to be an adult is before adulthood starts.* It defies common sense to doubt that the excitement of tuning in to one's calling is more absorbing than gadgets and screens. We draw that conclusion only because most boys have never been given the option to do something truly interesting and challenging, *guided by supervision.*

Very young children wake up excited to be *doing.* This is the natural human condition, and effective schools build on that momentum, at least until middle school. With respect to older boys, there is an urgent need to address their frequent loss of vigor, momentum, and authorship. Shouldn't this be a priority in a world overwhelmed by a need for people who can make a difference?

Work Develops Citizenship

If being educated is relevant to becoming a good citizen, then work must be included in that equation. Working is a basic expression of citizenship for nearly everybody. In the early US colonies, men were unwelcome unless they could do something useful. Usefulness was a great source of pride; it was the most basic requirement for joining a community. Today in society at large, the possibility of life-affirming work is viewed more like a lottery than the culmination of insight and thoughtful decision-making. The winners in this lottery will get work they love, and the rest will presumably soldier on as best they can — accepting the prevailing notion that work is personally irrelevant, a lifelong burden which no one can escape. Incredibly, if a boy feels at odds with this bleak scenario, it may be described simply as "growing pains": "He doesn't understand adulthood yet." This current view of the relationship between work and life is totally unacceptable. It's a bigger problem than electronics, fast food, or rampant marijuana use. Huge numbers of young people are up life's river without any practical paddles. How can we allow this to continue?

Urgency and Necessity

As hard as it is to motivate boys to take work seriously, there are two factors which help greatly: *urgency and necessity*. These factors add up to a feeling that something important needs to be accomplished right away. In most boys' lives, there is a striking absence of urgency and necessity. The closest most get is a deadline for a school assignment. And this is more a source of stress than excitement. Urgency and necessity elevate the status of work, making it something worthwhile, and prospectively, impressive to others. There are boys who can create their own internal urgency, and who have the discipline to follow that call. For the clear majority, however, there is a need to join some type of group effort: a call to action made by someone who commands their influence. A call that activates strength and honor — *the strength to do what's right, and the honor to do it well.*

For most young people, there is no pressing need to do one thing over another thing. Much of Western culture revolves around the idea of "do whatever makes you feel good." This might seem like freedom, but its effect is a subtle nihilism in which nothing matters enough to supersede simply having fun. Boys are experts at wasting time on a wide range of pixelated fun. Don't get me wrong. Fun is essential, and I'm not fanatically opposed to electronica. But there is a broad need for more purposeful fun, so that boys have a more balanced relationship with their environments. The best opportunities for purposeful work are found near home, although sometimes being supervised by a parent doesn't work so well. Boys can sometime hear an extended family member, and others in the community, with more clarity. As you probably know, family dynamics have a way of adding an unwanted layer of emotional conflict.

I have known many boys from affluent families who travelled far and wide to participate in noble, purposeful work. That's great if you have the resources, but the effect of many of those efforts could have been achieved more simply. Although I'm advocating activities that begin at home or in the community, the work must be more than a chore. It's positive when young people contribute to an environmental initiative (such as picking up community litter) or help with social services (such as participating in a food drive). Clearly, these are positive contributions. Yet chores and most volunteer activities do not provide the kind of personal, transformative experience that work does. An exception is when the task and goals are authored by the boy; examples include a 13-year-old who takes charge of how the driveway will be shoveled or assumes responsibility for setting up a cookout.

Work is how boys and young men make a place for themselves in the world. With urgency and necessity, emotion is attached to a task, making it more stimulating and motivating. It seems wrong to create emergencies out of nothing. Such an effort would be absurd, and immediately transparent to boys. We can, however, ask boys to help solve serious problems — problems that affect people in serious ways, and which call for practical action. And we can bring a sense of urgency to such projects through our tone, management of time, explanation of objectives, and persistent seriousness. The gravity of our own bearing is what attracts boys to work with us; it holds their attention.

The most formative challenge in preparing the current generation to do purposeful work is building their capacity to attach to work. I don't mean to encourage workaholism. Attaching to work means discovering a part of yourself in the work you do. There may be no better place for that attachment to grow than in a close relationship of uncompromised hope between adult and child. In the simplest terms: *ideal work* is first imagined and desired for a child by the *ideal parent* or *ideal teacher*. Hoping for a child to have good and purposeful work is an expression of unconditional love that nurtures a child's self-regard; it supports that individual's belief that he is worthy of such work. This journey begins in childhood, and warrants much attention in adolescence when goals and ideals are being formed. Stay close, and keep talking.

Remember

- Purposeful work is transformative because it elevates feelings of competence, contribution, and skillfulness.
- Boys define themselves and uncover elements of authenticity through work.
- Because most boys confuse work with chores, few have ever felt the interest and joy of personally relevant work.
- Mentors make purposeful work possible. Without supervision, guidance, and encouragement, purposeful work will not move beyond being an ideal for most.

Points to Consider

- What can you practically do to create opportunities for purposeful work?
- Have you thought about the kinds of work that seem to be a good fit for the boy in question?
- Are you resolved to let him do work that is nonpaying, without making your concern about that his concern?
- Is it OK for him to struggle with work that is somewhat ambitious or difficult?

Chapter 8

Keys to Motivation

IMAGINE THAT WE WERE TO CONVENE a meeting of parents and teachers from around the world and ask them about their top frustrations with boys. There is no doubt that concern about limited motivation would be near the top of the list. It seems like every group I present to, and almost every family I meet with in my office, voice some complaint about a lack of motivation in boys. This can become a major source of family tension, often leading to loud arguments and hurt feelings. There are some practical reasons for this concern which I will address in this chapter, and there are also some deep misunderstandings about what motivation is and where it comes from.

Adults become frustrated trying to motivate boys when we jump in to solve a problem without an accurate or adequate understanding of the psychology of motivation. My writing in this chapter, as in previous chapters, is not an academic summary of research on motivation, but draws from experience working to help boys overcome *inertia* that often takes hold during adolescence. This includes a lazy malaise some parents observe in their sons, which seems to attack determination, and even optimism.

My objective is to help reframe your thoughts about how people are best motivated, and to provide practical skills for helping the important boys in your life. I am less focused on helping you to be a taskmaster, more focused on showing you how to help boys discover and engage their own momentum. When we work to help uncover key sources of momentum, we allow motivation to sustain itself. This is stronger than motivation shaped by threats or incentives. First, we need to understand why motivation is such a huge dilemma for so many boys.

Why Motivation Is a Challenge

Basically, boys resist motivation because of the stress involved in trying very hard at something. This principle applies to all kinds of tasks, even those of obvious value. When the person to be motivated is already pushing up against the limits of his capability, the effort required is even more stressful — inherently unpleasant. Compounding the situation is that the spectator culture so many boys live in provides a parallel universe in which excitement and rewards can be found easily and vicariously. For many, that excitement is so intense that there is no apparent reason to move outside of the spectator universe. When I talk to boys about their virtual experiences, I hear that the victories and accomplishments they achieve feel real and consequential. For example, there is massive pride conveyed by a 7-year-old in the construction of a great Minecraft world, and triumph enjoyed by 16-year-olds in combat-simulation games. By contrast, their everyday life might feel dramatically bland. This contrast speaks to a core issue of motivation and why it is important for boys to be their own lead explorer in a quest for life momentum.

As adults, we may reason that effort is how one ensures success in life. But for boys, success seems elusive and distant. The results that flow from their efforts often feel personally unsatisfying. This problem is related to another fundamental challenge of motivation — much of life, as it is presented to boys, is highly uninteresting! Is it hard for you to believe that after all you do to provide the best quality of life imaginable for your son, it is often unappreciated? Regrettably, this is the case. *Much of what boys value has more to do with happiness than success.* Yet much of what adults want for boys is behavior that is goal-directed, aimed at success.

Whose Idea Is This?

Compounding this problem is our tendency as adults is to make so many things obligatory. Our demands are met by natural skepticism and resistance. So often, our suggestions are transparent efforts toward character building. It's not that character is unimportant. But boys have little patience with overt gestures toward building morals and character — especially because it is almost always done from an adult perspective. The resulting conflict isn't really a difference in logical priorities; it's more an emotional conflict about who's in charge. We may be able to impose our values easily in childhood, but it's much harder to do so during adolescence. In some cases, boys' resistance leads to emotional paralysis which we might think of as the "malaise" of adolescence. Boredom, distraction, and lethargy can cause the whole mind-body system to be sluggish. Inertia might set in, and then it feels hard for a boy to do anything.

Happiness vs. Success

Some boys become deflated by life itself, by the impossibility of serving different goals, especially the dichotomy between happiness and success. For many, happiness is about living in the moment and doing what feels good right now. Success, as most of us could agree, is somewhat the opposite. It implies living for the future, and delaying gratification for the sake of longer-term rewards — what I've termed an "investment" approach to life. Can you see the dilemma in this scenario? If we ask boys to delay gratification in favor of what the future holds, they are naturally inclined to consider what they see in the future. I'm afraid that most do not see a world of adults consumed by happiness. Instead, they see a world dominated by obligation and routine, absent the spontaneity and exuberance that comes so easily in youth.

My own beliefs about the challenge of motivating boys have changed over time. In the early years of my career, my tendency was to join with the frustration of parents, and in turn to be very parent-like in my conversations with boys. In those days, I spent most of my time trying to help boys understand the consequences of their actions. My principle goal was to help them make better decisions, which I understood to be decisions that would lead to longer-term rewards. But over time I've come to understand the emotionally unsatisfying, low return on that approach. I've learned that *you can't help boys to find momentum until you have found some compassion for the difficulty of being oneself.* The greatest achievement in living is learning how to be yourself, while also being responsible.

We adults struggle with the happiness-success divide as well, but we become clever at burying our feelings about this dilemma so that we can be sufficiently productive and satisfy others. Is this our philosophy of the good life, or a rationalization based on perceived roadblocks? Please think about this idea and how it is relevant to your own relationship with boys. And please think about how to listen more deeply than you ever have. We convey respect for boys and deepen our relationship when we can empathize with their values.

I know that some may be thinking that I simply don't understand their son or their students. You may be thinking of a boy who seems impossible to help, who doesn't want to relate, and who resists any offer of empathy. I know these boys exist in significant numbers, and they test our patience. When the conversation gets personal, however, I hear that relatively few boys lack interest in their own authenticity. Probing for authenticity creates trust and a working alliance — the sense that happiness is at the center of the conversation. Of course this requires a willingness to take the priorities of boys seriously, and to help them move toward what they value.

What Do We Mean by Motivation?

Let's honestly address what we mean by motivation, and then consider the consequences. Do we mean:

> **A.** Helping young people to discover what naturally excites them, activating mind, body, and a sense of purpose?
>
> **B.** Getting kids to do what does not interest or excite them?

I'm guessing that many of us mean B. Let's admit this to ourselves. We want to get young people excited about doing things which do not necessarily interest them. Most of us will agree that personal responsibility is a highly valued indication of maturity. It sets the tone for how many parents relate to their children. At some point, every adolescent inspires a basic question: how close is this person to assuming responsibility for his own life? That concern prompts us to motivate those whose lives seem stalled, or who are genuinely uninterested in responsibility. We operate with the belief that stalled momentum cries out for inspiration and direction.

Yet the mistake in our thinking is this: *true motivation is never inspired.*

Most boys are wary of those who seek to orchestrate their will. No matter how it might be intended, an intention to motivate is ultimately a desire to co-opt someone else's personal priorities. It is unavoidably contentious because it pits one person's will against another's.

Traditional approaches to motivation are more applicable to military service or sports; these are contexts where vigorous compliance and commitment to a specific outcome is essential to victory. But motivating someone to "grow up" is considerably more complicated. Adults and adolescents don't necessarily agree on what merits effort or what being "grown up" looks like. This dilemma underscores how supremely difficult it is to make someone want what they don't already desire. But is this really a problem, or simply a testament to human resilience? And could this resistance even be a prized personality trait? Isn't this another way of saying "strong willed?" Certainly, and that's not all bad.

It's no secret that appropriated ideas are second nature to a generation that grew up surfing information online, *a circuit with no defined beginning or end.* What is less understood is how cultivated distraction implicitly challenges goal-directedness. *For boys coming of age now, the linear effort of goal-directed thought is much less pleasurable than mentally floating from one focal point to the next.* This shift has less to do with a wish to upend a traditional understanding of attention, than an impulse for more immediate satisfaction.

The reason it's so hard to break away from surfing the net is that being in a real-time loop of virtual experience feels like participating, even when you're only spectating. The objective of the loop is not necessarily to master what one reads, so much as it is to keep up. This net-surfing effect poses a unique challenge: how do we motivate a generation whose momentum is more reactive than proactive? Does motivation have relevance for boys who have abandoned traditional perspectives of progress? So many young men live for the moment, seemingly unaware of the longer-term consequences of having no life plan. Although adult concern is warranted, we must tread carefully, or we become part of an ignored chorus of negativity.

Don't Try to Fool Boys

Boys can be incredibly sophisticated about being passive and bored as a way of shielding themselves from enthusiasms we try to impose on them. Teenagers have a sixth sense for coercion, no matter how well it is disguised.

> "Let's vacuum the downstairs so the house looks good when your friends arrive."
> "My friends don't care how the house looks. Their houses are worse. I'll tell them not to look at the floor."

Boys seem to know when emotion is being used to ensnare them in a situation that is not of their own making. My clinical work requires me to wrestle with this problem. I sympathize with boys who don't want to be led by someone else's priorities. At the same time, my belief in the benefits of *feeling motivated* is unequivocal. Why? Because motivated people almost always appear to be a little happier than others; they typically convey an attachment to some sort of goal or belief that gives life purpose and direction. Those benefits aside, the turbulence of becoming motivated is considerable. To go from being unmotivated to motivated is like turning oneself inside out. It demands flexibility, critical analysis of oneself, and a tolerance for discomfort. Most seriously, it usually means adopting values that are not one's own.

It's not that the unmotivated don't, or wouldn't, enjoy feeling otherwise. No matter how skillful the motivator, a small part of every healthy soul is opposed to submission. Adolescence puts that opposition on steroids. The resistance may surface as debate, procrastination, or outright refusal. Yet the underlying sentiment is much the same: nothing alien to "me" should inhabit "my" passions and effort. A boy's basic instinct for self-preservation prevents him from wanting to be occupied in that way.

> When we try too hard to motivate boys it feels like an invasion. Our enthusiasm is not the same as their enthusiasm. Sometimes overt motivation feels like a *hostile takeover.*

Motivation Is Emotional and Personal

The overtures of adults fail because we don't see how *motivation is an emotional transaction.* The best teachers and therapists understand this principle well. Basically, boys allow themselves to be genuinely motivated (meaning they accept some degree of excitement) when they believe the activity or result will be personally satisfying. When they don't connect with that emotional reward, they may still do what is asked, but only out of obligation or fear of reprimand. That is not motivation.

True motivation activates a boy's sense of *congruity* — the feeling that one's actions are consistent with one's core self. Congruity makes us feel more attuned to those things we value most. This could be our most prized personality traits, recreational interests, social or political values. Boys want others, especially parents, to recognize these differences — and honor them in relationships, communication, and teaching.

It feels good when someone tries to nurture congruity. That's why athletes submit to half-time pep talks, and why executives are stirred by the words of an executive coach. The person being motivated has faith that the advice will yield a *personally desirable* (congruent) outcome. By extension, apprehension is disarmed. This is good because occasionally boys need to be curious and confident as much as they need to feel motivated. *Ultimately, feeling motivated is a way of belonging to the world.* The feeling of acceleration which motivation sparks is advantageous and

> **Basic fact of life:** the most spirited tend to be eager to "cure" the less spirited, even though their attempts at healing share a faulty, unarticulated premise: "be more like me and less like you."

fun. Think about how being motivated goes along with feeling optimistic and capable. It's all good.

It's not strategic to attempt to take over someone else's will aggressively. Between parent and child, it marginalizes appreciation of what a boy wants for himself, and it is easily detected by even the most inattentive adolescent. Many of us worry constantly about what boys are doing or thinking! In the US, it has become a national obsession. Many adults plainly struggle with the high priority most boys place on gratification. For example, our goals don't have much to do with adolescent priorities like having fun, being sexual, and wanting ample time for relaxation.

Adolescence loves rapture, but has a more contentious relationship with responsibility. It's a conflict that must run its course — although there's no real consensus on where the course ends.

Adult Expectations May Be Unrealistic

As the pace of daily life accelerates, the image we hold for able-bodied teenagers looks much more like mania than relaxed poise. We want boys to exude energy, and project a "can-do" attitude. It may not occur to us to consider that our infatuation with energy may express unspoken fears. For example, will my lethargic, seemingly lazy son be left behind socially and economically? Does he lack a larger life purpose? *Perpetual energy can be an attractive substitute for meaning.* Energized people personify notions of success; a boy's busyness may relieve our concern that he lacks specific goals. Hey, at least he's doing something, right?

The contrast between adult expectations of teens and younger children is striking. While we want older boys to be busy and focused, we may complain that younger children are busy beyond reason. In some ways, railing against busyness is a reactive way of expressing identification with wholesome values. Consider the common refrain, "let children be children." Are we then going to extend the same latitude to adolescents? Those who feel obligated to defend the absolute freedom of childhood may be unlikely to have their own languishing, ear-budded teenagers in mind when they do so.

Although young people are unlikely to fully understand the worry of those who raise them, it's not as though they don't feel the effects of those concerns. The stress of being a 21st-century teenager in North America and elsewhere is enormous, and frequently has a paradoxical effect on teen behavior. Instead of boosting productive activity, stress contributes to withdrawal and, in some cases, stagnation. The result can be inertia. This is the most difficult aspect of what is called ADHD; boys between 13 and 15 can be really dug in, essentially hibernating, hoping the stress will pass.

Are We Diagnosing the Problem Correctly?

There are no medical cures for a boy who finds school or entry-level jobs intolerably dull. For many, *distraction is essentially an unwillingness to sit attentively in classrooms and jump through hoops of accomplishment that have been defined by someone else.* Woodworker Doug Stowe, who blogs daily, advocating for more hands-on opportunity for young people, suggests school is not living up to student expectations. Stowe correctly indicates that students often think to themselves "what's in it for me?"[5] If you're thinking these terms apply only to the few, I humbly ask you to consult your nearest high school.

In my own research, boys robustly express their belief that the way to discover one's interests and talents is by trying new things. Yet "new things" are conspicuously absent in many young people's lives, including school. Matthew Crawford notes that "reclaiming the real" is essential to making education more relevant. Crawford suggests we need "to understand that one is educating a person who is situated in the world and orients to it through a set of human concerns."[6] Amen! Let's stop the emphasis on abstractions, and help boys move into more pragmatic, and consequential relationships with the world. Think: *community, scale of endeavor, significant events.*

Inertia amplifies boys' uncertainty about what's worth doing. As a result, many boys are unsure of the best path to happiness. Just a few generations ago, happiness wouldn't have been thought of as something one had to plan for, so much as the effect of a life well lived. But today, many young people have become lost in too many possibilities about how to allocate their time. That may sound good on the surface, but underneath it leads to more confusion and anxiety than pleasure. No one wishes for a life of hardship, yet limitations have a way of making the lunge for escape feel exciting.

A person freed from all risk and responsibility is cast adrift, with no urgency to row this way or that. As with the vast galaxy of internet amusement, their life amounts to an endless circling of possibilities with no important destination.

We can better understand the dilemma of adolescents if we see its corollary in the work world. Being a competent worker is rarely enough for an employer; most employees are also expected to carry out their job with a proper disposition. The suppression of selfhood is a compromise one often makes to be gainfully employed. It's an expectation of virtually everyone who works — equally true of a retail manager, an offshore teletech, and an actor working a day job. Even where organizations invite free thinking, there is an implicit expectation that those free thoughts will be focused on the well-being of the organization.

This is the dilemma that stirs late adolescence, and which is foreshadowed by the experience of going to school. Boys are surrounded by energy and positive emotion, but the problem is that *much of that enthusiasm is not of their own making.* The hesitation and inertia that young people experience in response to this situation is a way of resisting other people's priorities.

Many boys are hunkered down, unwilling to concede to the attitude and emotional suppression they are supposed to demonstrate as signs of maturity. Many of us might agree that resistance is not in a boy's long-term interest, but that's not the main concern of a young person who has discovered personal power through passive resistance. If a person sinks deep enough into rebellion, it becomes familiar and comfortable. It's perilously hard to talk a boy out of that situation.

Solution: go in the other direction as early as possible. Challenge a boy to find fulfillment and authenticity. This is a practical way of showing love and demonstrating respect. It doesn't mean boys' lives will go off the rails; it just means you are willing to trust the process of allowing a boy to become himself. And by the way, this needs to be made clear in words. It's not enough to think these thoughts, without somehow expressing them.

Searching for Congruity

So, do young people affected by refusal, or at least hesitation, have irreconcilable differences with the world beyond themselves? The best hope for an energized, motivated life is to make *congruence* the centerpiece — the main project. This approach doesn't necessarily require the pursuit of personal fantasies, but it does require building a life around what one enjoys, and identifies with. Belief in that possibility allows boys to be motivated naturally. And the absence of this belief is the essence of the motivation gap — the distance between merely thinking and doing.

Annually, a small army of new college grads marches forward with the hope that their work and life will, in some meaningful way, reflect their educational choices. Opportunity to pursue happiness through vocation is essential because more routine forms of contentment — especially those derived from self-reliance — have been in steep decline for decades. Few of us in North America live lives that include any sense of hands-on urgency or necessity. For most in this society, *self-reliance has evolved to mean earning enough money to sustain whatever lifestyle a person wants.* Yet there is still a considerable gap between that achievement and a congruent life: a situation where our work matches our core interests and values. Pursuit of a better coordinated, fulfilling life expresses belief in the capacity of work to be transcendent. Boys dream of interesting, important work. In such work, they find reason and reward — a way out of inertia and toward a more sustainable happiness.

External vs. Internal Motivation

It's important to understand that a fire ignited from within burns longer than one sparked by external rewards. This means motivation burns brightest and longest when it comes from personal interest and enthusiasm, rather than external rewards. Unfortunately, the most common

approaches to motivating boys organize systems for rewarding good behavior. What message do we send adolescents and young adults when
we reinforce behavior, without considering whether a person feels motivated inside? I'm concerned that a big take-home message for boys
is that compliance is more important than a passion. Can this message conceivably encourage happiness or true motivation? Certainly,
middle-aged workers want more meaningful acknowledgment than
the approval of having successfully followed work protocols. Similarly,
young people need to have their selves recognized apart from any civil,
compliant behavior they demonstrate at home and school.

The Keys to Motivation (In order of priority)

1. Urgency and Necessity

Of all the factors most likely to influence boys to act, urgency and necessity reign supreme. It's hard to imagine that anything could cause a
greater surge in adrenaline than the feeling that something important
is happening now. It's too contrived to construct an urgent situation.
So, we have to look around and see what important things need to be
done. This need not be an emergency with potentially catastrophic consequences. It does have to be deadline driven, or feel like it is an action
that warrants more immediate attention. Several examples of urgency
and necessity include: harvesting fruit or vegetables before they rot; participating in a community action to improve a bad situation; acting to
protect someone, especially at school; providing an essential service. As
powerful as urgency and necessity can be, they are time-limited. Where
we seek motivation to be of a more enduring nature we must look to
congruity.

2. Congruity

This is where the rubber meets the road in boys' lives. Congruity defines
where it's time to stop fooling around with activities and abstractions
that are peripheral to one's genuine, authentic interests. A congruent
life means you feel at home in your reality, and that your effort and
work are guided towards something of personal relevance and value.
This is powerful stuff! It is the sort of life boys want in adulthood, but

which they doubt is truly possible. Looking around at what others are doing, they fear life is destined to be a repetitive cycle of subordination and boredom for pay. Youth is the time to correct this perception. There is no time to waste because such perceptions become locked in by adolescence. All kinds of decisions are being made about post-secondary study based on assumptions about what work is, and how someone will receive their pay. Think big. Don't be afraid to let your pre-adolescent son envision a project of some scale — something ambitious enough to impress friends, family, and neighbors. Think about the value of a skilled practice — the antidote to living inside your head.

3. Clarity of Purpose

It's hard to make any headway in the world if you don't know what it is that you're working on. It is tragic that the average high school student has no real sense of purpose. We do not magically find motivation when adulthood emerges. Purposeful people have an inclination toward momentum early on in their lives. If we treat boys as though they are too young or immature to have a purpose, they will use that perception as an excuse for delaying the mental work of determining what is important to them. This process of clarification can be a dialogue that goes on at home, over the course of years. It might begin by helping boys to understand what they stand for, but it must then transition to how one's identity can serve a call larger than himself. This is how we build strength and honor. Please don't misunderstand me. I'm not suggesting that every boy wants to become invested in a large social purpose, will want to defend his country, or will in some way want to act as a change agent in the world. But I am suggesting that whatever one decides to do, it needs to be articulated and planned for, because that's how dreams and aspirations become reality.

4. Do Things Together

When all else fails and your son won't get off the sofa, when he won't engage no matter what inspiration or rationalization you provide, your best option is to do something *with him*. Partnership provides a foundation that is more grounded than words alone. When you do something with another person you must respond to them, and think about the elements of collaboration. It's less difficult to see the beginning and end of a task when you're working with someone else. It's more fun. There's more communication. You are in the same mental orbit with another person, and thus feel less lonely. If you have existential doubts (why am I doing this?), they can be helped by the companionship, focus, and energy of a partner. Sometimes, it is while doing things together that we find answers to other questions as well. I have suggested that the best conversations with boys happen as a background to another activity that feels purposeful. Where that activity involves learning practical skills — which are inherently life affirming — it's even better.

5. Structure Time and Effort

Sometimes our expectations of boys feel too large, with parameters that are too vague. In such cases, break it down. In fact, you almost can't break it down enough. Break every task down into a series of chunks. Identify how much time will be needed to complete each chunk, when specific actions will take place, and any materials you'll need. Intervening to work out something together is how we help boys affected by the great inertia. I'm talking about those boys who don't budge as we hurl out our best inspirational ideas. These are boys who have a constant poker face, disaffected by seemingly everything; they appear allergic to ambition. Almost always, a boy who needs structured time and effort will also benefit from partnership. I believe we should have great compassion for boys stuck in this rut. When I recommend structuring time and effort, I don't mean we should behave like prison guards structuring afternoon recreation in the prison yard. Structure need not preclude doing things that are interesting and exciting — for example, activities that might help a boy discover a sense of himself. Yet for those who struggle the most with motivation, clear delineation of steps involved in any task at hand is much appreciated.

6. Only Privileges, No Bribes

Regarding younger boys, we sometimes wonder how to reward them for making constructive changes in their behavior. I try to avoid reward systems in my clinical practice because I think they can reinforce immaturity. Rewards have an unfortunate way of trivializing relationships with kids, distracting us from the more interesting and important work of building self-knowledge. However, I realize that five-, six-, and seven-year-olds can be activated by constructive rewards. In those cases, I make two strong recommendations:

1. Never organize a system where a child starts out with some form of "capital" and then has it gradually removed as he makes mistakes. This is humiliating and reinforces your power to punish, more than it excites boys to work toward something positive. The reward is best given as it is earned.

2. I strongly recommend that rewards be related to privileges and some degree of status, rather than some objects. It's a counterproductive and unsustainable to get boys in the habit of getting a new toy for good behavior. It's not a good idea to be running to the store every time a child has remembered to brush his teeth or has stopped fighting with his sister. Privileges suggest status, and help a boy to define his identity and preferences. They are a more sustainable and psychologically beneficial reward.

I hope you leave this chapter recognizing that motivation has more dimensions than most of us assume. With respect to boys, it's more than a matter of knowing the right thing to say, or providing the right incentive. Remember the essential distinction between motivation and coercion. Motivation helps a person discover those things in life that excite and activate him; it is not about figuring out how to get someone to do what he dislikes. We all do things out of obligation, and the best framing for such obligations is *responsibility*. It is true that all boy's lives involve necessary activities, about which they may be less than enthusiastic. But in almost every circumstance I can recall, an element of interest or relevance can make almost any task more interesting. Sometimes the context of a task needs elaboration, and at other times it is mostly a matter of decreasing the loneliness of facing what's perceived as a big hurdle. There are other circumstances as well, those involving personal doubt, sadness, anxiety, or bad habits. These are among the challenges I want to discuss next in addressing psychotherapy with boys.

Remember

- Motivation is more emotional than analytical. It needs to draw upon personal sources of interest and excitement.
- Adults and boys have different ideas about what merits effort. *Before you set an agenda,* take time to consider potential differences.
- Boys will feel more motivated by tasks that seem consequential beyond their own lives. The constant admonishment to simply "try harder" usually kills motivation.

Points to Consider

- Do you know what excites the relevant boy in your life? Have you learned this by talking, or only observing?
- Are you projecting your own productivity anxieties onto your son?
- Does his daily routine need a reset? Without new experiences, it's hard to discover new paths of interest.
- Is there something two or more people could do together as a means of greater momentum, and a more significant memory?

Chapter 9

Therapy with Boys

M OST READERS WILL HAVE SURMISED that the concerns addressed in this book could be the focus of psychotherapy with boys. In fact, therapy is where most of my insight comes from. As a psychologist, I have a strong belief in the merits of the therapeutic relationship. My perspective is broader than the notion of counseling to fix a short-term problem. There are many issues that benefit from a more in-depth relationship that unfolds over time. Time allows the fullness of each boy's mind and voice to emerge. This becomes the foundation of confidence and strength we all hope to see in boys.

In Chapter 9, I want to discuss those elements of therapy that I've found to be especially helpful in *building an alliance* between boys and adults, and which have proven to be effective in *producing positive outcomes.* These two things go together. A good alliance goes a long way toward ensuring a positive outcome. As I explained in Part I, there is no element of relationship more powerful than tone. This awareness is foremost in my mind when I meet a child for the first time. After I've reviewed referral notes collected by my office, but before I have met a boy, I think about how I want to present myself. It's important to create positive energy in the first minute of an initial encounter. In seeking a therapist for your own child, I encourage you to consider someone who projects an authoritative and constructive vocal tone.

Therapy is organic, and things may happen during treatment which change the approach. A child in tears, or one so overcome by anxiety that he cannot speak, of course inspires a softer tone. Rarely, however, is there justification for not being friendly and positive. This attitude is conveyed by voice, facial expressions, and physical greetings such as a handshake. In my office, the very short walk between the waiting room and consulting room is an important transition for a child and family. For one, the spaces look notably different, with my consulting room being full of activities and home-like furniture. Many kids say, "this is like a house," an observation that is enhanced by the gabled ceiling, soft lighting, comfortable furniture, and wood floor.

Being welcoming and optimistic makes the transition into the consulting room easier. Although this transition may be a relief for stressed adults, for boys there is apprehension. For some, it feels like a descent into a place of interrogation or punishment. Because of my expertise in boys' communication, I am visited by many who struggle with social communication. Can you think of the last place on earth you want to be if you are a boy struggling with social communication? You guessed it: meeting with someone like me. Naturally, it feels a little like a punishment, and it's not uncommon that I encounter a glum face in the waiting room during an initial visit.

Before I get into specific elements of treatment, let me describe finding a suitable therapist. Sometimes it's helpful for parents to interview a therapist before treatment starts. This gives you a chance to convey sensitive concerns privately, and helps the therapist better understand the issues involved. The more difficult challenge is knowing which therapist to choose. My best advice is to ask others who have sought treatment for a child about their experiences. If you have no starting point at all, asking a school counselor for a referral is a good idea. Independent schools often invest considerable effort into developing a network of providers, and they may be willing to share a name or two, even if your child does not attend the school.

Sometimes people believe that children are widely understood by psychologists and therapists, but in my experience, many people in mental health find young people to be a mystery — and less interesting to work with than adults. So, make sure you identify someone that has considerable experience with young people, and who really enjoys child and adolescent therapy. Unfortunately, there is typically no list of clinicians specializing in work with boys. People frequently contact me seeking a referral for a therapist in their community. Alas, at present, no such resource exists. Asking people in your community is the best option.

First Meeting

There are two primary objectives in an initial evaluation. First, it is important to collect relevant information about the perceived problem, as well as its origins and effects. Second, it is essential to plant the seeds of relationship. I like to think that this process begins in the waiting room during the greeting. Certainly, it begins as soon as everyone sits down in the consulting room, and we begin to unfold different perspectives on "the problem." Almost always, boys under age 19 are accompanied by at least one parent. Sometimes boys feel confident in relating the specifics of a problem, but often they prefer that a parent introduce the key issues. Many are self-conscious about whatever the problem is, and have often pleaded with a parent not to say certain things during the appointment.

Clearly, there are elements of a person's life that feel embarrassing. If you are nine and still occasionally wet the bed, you probably don't want a stranger to know. Just as if you're 17 and have been expelled for selling an ADHD stimulant at school, you're not thrilled about reliving the facts with people who "totally don't get how normal this is." Parents always explain that the family has come for help, and "we have to tell everything." Boys typically grimace and avoid eye contact when they hear this. I usually feel like this is my first opportunity to normalize the process of therapy, and the idea that every life involves occasional challenges.

Employing task tone, and remaining very matter of fact, I begin to ask a few questions about the issue at hand. When did it begin? Why are you seeking help now? What sort of outcome are you hoping for? How badly do you want to fix this? Throughout this back-and-forth exchange it's helpful to maintain an emotionally neutral disposition. A workman-like attitude reassures boys. When boys feel particularly self-conscious about a problem, they assume that others will be shocked when they hear about it. Avoiding a shocked response goes a long way toward signaling that the problem is normal and manageable.

If a parent has been doing all the explaining about a particular concern, it's a good idea to check in with the child to determine if he agrees. This typically happens within the first 20 minutes of an initial meeting. Then it's time to begin a deeper phase of relationship-building. This is accomplished by addressing questions directly to the child. Even a boy as young as five or six can respond reasonably well to a series of clear, answerable questions. My approach to this task might seem counterintuitive to you. For example, rather than using a quiet, slow, therapist voice, I speak more rapidly, asking successive questions, each of which is easy to answer. It's useful to use forced choice questions at this point in the encounter, like: So, do you fight more with your brother or kids at school? What do you do after school? Do you feel more worried at night or in the morning? What do you usually eat for lunch? Which is your favorite Pokémon? Is it more difficult for you to understand math or remember what you have read?

As I'm asking these questions, many families assume that the questions themselves are the point of the dialogue. Certainly, this is what boys assume. It's true that information is being collected which may be useful in formulating an approach to treatment. *But the real value of this early interaction is the formation of relationship.*

Few of us have any idea how relieving it is for boys to be asked a series of answerable questions. Substantial confidence grows from this type of rapport. Not only is the boy meeting the interviewer's expectations, maintaining pace and staying with the flow, but he's also doing this in front of parents. This is often impressive, if not astounding, to parents who are accustomed to long silences in conversations with their sons. The subtext of this interaction is "See how easy this is? We're going to get along well."

The second message of this exchange is to reinforce who the client is. Once boys get over their apprehension about the burdens of being a client, a sense of importance and specialness can develop out of such interaction. This includes an attachment to the space in which the initial conversation takes place — the consulting office. Positive early associations are encouraging waypoints in an unfolding journey.

An effective first meeting includes some feedback from the therapist about the problem, and the prospects for solving it. This attitude is not universally accepted in psychotherapy. In my own training, I was taught not to get caught up in solving a person's problem, but instead to guide them toward a decision or actions of their own conception. While this may work for some adults, it's generally not a good approach with young people. It may have the unfortunate effect of making therapy circular. It's not helpful to keep bringing boys back to how they "feel about the problem." Clarity about optimal outcomes propels progress and reduces anxiety. It's impossible to overstate the importance of speaking the truth. One can be serious without being negative or worrisome. Seriousness feels honest. It builds trust. It's important to provide both child and family with a sense of what will be helpful and why. Such advice changes not only from one problem to the next, but also from one boy to the next.

Setting

The most important aspect of the therapy setting is comfort. The consultation room should feel welcoming, with comfortable seating, and ample space for various activities. Boys are keenly aware of possibilities for engagement as they scan the therapy office. It's best not to hide games and related activities in containers or closets, but place them prominently on a worktable or elsewhere. There is a bit of staging involved here, and the activities need to be appealing and relatable. For this reason, I always put out action figures, stuffed animals for the youngest children, and interesting artwork to appeal to older kids. It's not uncommon for parents to be "all business" at the first meeting, but boys are very observant of the space and "what goes on here."

It's clear when you enter my office that this is a "maker's space." The room accommodates a large wooden table suitable for all kinds of games, including kinetic activities that might involve building things, using light tools, or occasionally doing art or written work. The space needs to be set up to allow for ample movement. This atmosphere communicates "BOYS WELCOME HERE." Frequently, kids want to roll, jump, or move about as we are talking about various topics. It's helpful to be sensitive to the height at which items are placed on the floor so that four- and five-year-old children will be able to reach some things on their own. A strategic element of building an alliance with a child is to ask him to retrieve a specific toy or game, and to set it up in a particular way. Securing this type of cooperation goes a long way toward framing an authoritative relationship in which it is possible to ask boys to apply effort toward identified goals.

Fun, Interest, and Support

Most therapists work with a range of ages. It's not uncommon for someone to be skilled at working with younger children, as well as tweens and teens. The operative element in establishing momentum and positive rapport with younger boys is a powerful sense of fun. This is initially communicated by the presence of appealing activities. The critical element for older boys is interesting content. This is best communicated in the first meeting, and is conveyed by speaking the truth, and focusing on issues that are of greatest relevance to boys themselves. This can be tricky because it's easy to get caught up in the concerns of parents or schools, losing sight of what is relevant to the child. It's not that the concerns of others are unimportant, or will not be addressed, but if a boy's interest in the process is not activated in the initial meeting, then success is less certain.

A first impression is hugely important. Knowing something about the activities that interest adolescent boys is essential. Better to go off on a tangent in the interest of building a relationship than drill down on a problem — especially in the early stages of therapy. *Boys change because they become intrinsically motivated to do so.* Feeling liked and respected helps to build that internal drive.

While games are important to younger boys, they are not the only element of therapy that builds relationship. Sometimes it is essential to join with the child, doing some type of labor or skilled task together. When meeting with very resistant boys, whom I've been told in advance are reluctant to meet me, I try to make an introduction of very few words. Almost as soon as we transition to the consulting room, I ask for help with a brief, physical task. This could be the moving of furniture, watering plants, or attending to my dog, Darcy. My goal here is to have a cooperative experience, and in some cases to establish the child's expertise about something.

Almost always, I ask boys to tell me what they know a lot about. It doesn't matter to me whether it is family, school, Minecraft, or lacrosse. What matters is that their voice is being heard as a source of opinion and expertise. Boys need to get used to leading a conversation and responding to questions. Again, the topic at hand is less critical than relationship building. When boys talk about those things they know well, the tempo becomes strong and the atmosphere is confident.

Although I use lots of games and art-making in my practice, I almost completely avoid so-called therapy games, like naming your feelings, or, "what makes you angry or sad." The intentions of such games are utterly transparent to boys, and few want to play along. These obvious attempts at psychoeducation are a poor substitute for therapeutic creativity and genuine engagement.

Inventive, spontaneous games and activities are a wonderful backdrop for the meaningful conversation that is the transformative experience of therapy. Whatever brings energy and momentum to that conversation is certainly an asset. Having an activity that stretches across multiple sessions is even more beneficial. It helps to sustain attention, and adds to the sense that the therapeutic relationship is building something over time.

Many of the activities in my office would likely be found in other psychotherapists' offices as well. However, I want to mention a few that I have found to be especially helpful with boys. Among other things, I've built a wooden track that allows for one or more small cars to be raced with only the aid of gravity. The track is an endless source of invention as it is used to span furniture, load toy trucks, and as a drag race strip. I also have an old-fashioned pinball-style baseball game which is loud and highly kinetic as the ball bangs around various game elements. My office contains numerous cars, trucks, and trains of all sizes. I have a unique and special set of hardwood blocks that enable the construction of absurdly high towers that can later be tipped over to create more calamitous fun. There is a beanbag chair for those who enjoy hurling themselves through space and onto a soft surface.

One of my most compelling tools is a microphone and small amplifier for broadcasting mock radio shows, in which the child is a "special guest." I have conducted hundreds of these mock broadcasts called

Lego® talk, Minecraft talk, Soccer talk, and so on. In each of these broadcasts, questions are posed by pretend callers (me), and boys are encouraged to share their perspective and expertise. Can you see the clear benefit of this task? My clinical work with boys began with the intent of improving social communication. That was almost my exclusive focus for several years. I've never lost appreciation for the value of enhancing social communication, and the microphone and amplifier are great at helping boys become comfortable with their own voice. This activity builds so much confidence and esteem that many kids have requested we do additional "shows" on subsequent visits.

Doing purposeful things, and having a structure for them, make a therapy meeting memorable. Along those lines, my office includes a bucket attached to a rope and pulley system. In the bucket, I keep snacks. The sharing of some simple food is helpful. It feels friendly and relaxed. It conveys good cheer. What's most important to boys is the untying of the rope, and the lowering of the bucket from the ceiling where it is hoisted. Then the bucket must be re-hoisted and re-tied. There is skill and confidence employed in this action. Also, I may be the only child therapist, anywhere, who keeps an antique railroad jack in his office. This 120-year-old jack can lift a 10-ton railroad car. It is also capable of hoisting me, and I have invited many boys to learn how to use the jack as a means of lifting me into the air. I can only imagine how this exercise must sound to you. The idea is to propel relationship and engagement in therapy. There is also the message that extraordinary things can be accomplished, even by the youngest people, when they have the right tools. When I sense that boys are attaching to me as their therapist, I know I have more influence in their lives. By extension, they are more invested in achieving the hoped-for outcome. Happiness and contentment between child and therapist is a foundation for the same elsewhere.

When it comes to connecting with teenagers, the activities I've been discussing are of little use. Instead, focusing on topics that emerge as high personal priorities propels the relationship and the possibilities of therapy. For this reason, I make a special effort to attend to whatever I discover is personally relevant to adolescent boys. I've done lots of sessions talking about surfing, music, sports, and electronic games. Every one of those topics suggests a depth of options for exploring life themes, conflict, and honor. Along with meeting boys at their points of interest, it's helpful to be a little provocative, and to touch upon issues that linger in boys' subconscious minds as important, but relatively unexplored. *My favorite topic, in this regard, is their authenticity because I believe many boys are at least subconsciously concerned with figuring out who they are.* There is often a strong, but unarticulated sense that making that discovery is essential to living a good life. Saying something about how such a process might be undertaken, and what the prospective benefits might be, is a great way to spark engagement.

Establishing *a holding environment*, a space and place in which support and patience remain constant despite the ups and downs of a day or week, is of immeasurable importance. This is the best way of normalizing emotional problems, and it is enhanced by using a task-tone. The notion of a holding environment is an old concept in psychotherapy, but I'm afraid that today it is underappreciated. It seems to be the intention of the health-insurance industry to have doctors and therapists shape treatment according to a person's benefits package, including making therapy as short-term as possible. These parameters undermine the development of a holding environment and the substantial emotional benefits derived from psychotherapy at greater depth.

While it may be necessary to cooperate with these limitations to enable treatment to go forward, it seems essential not to confuse these parameters with the actual structure of good treatment. Some therapy cases are inherently short-term, involving the resolution of a specific issue. Others, however, involve a longer arc of human growth. It is up to families to advocate for what is needed. This means seeing past the management of symptoms to the development of a whole person. That process requires a sustained holding environment and a therapeutic relationship that is long enough to be a significant chapter in a child's life. I've been fortunate to work with families that understand this dynamic. And so, we have persisted when things did not seem to be going well, when kids were resistant, and when everyone would have preferred to be at home doing something else. But in my desk, I keep a file of letters from young men whom I worked with when they were much younger, and more troubled. Those letters affirm the value of not giving up and the gratitude young men feel for having had a holding environment during the most challenging years of their lives.

Observable Outcomes

It's good practice to begin with the end in mind. Everybody feels more secure and less confused about therapy when there is a shared understanding of what is to be accomplished. This information is best clarified in the first meeting, but may be updated as therapy progresses. Because it is important for the child to be part of this *shared understanding*, it is also good practice to identify outcomes desirable to him. Further, by tying these goals to something that can be observed, there is proof that therapy has been effective. Defining observable outcomes goes a long way toward increasing the chances that those outcomes will be achieved. There is something uniquely valuable about creating a mental image of what success will look like. (This is part of why Individualized Educational Plans (IEPs) work well for schools.) Please understand that I am talking about more than a child's behavior. In my mind, the happiness of a boy is the most important outcome, because it is generally a foundation for anything else that might be accomplished.

Along these lines, therapy itself should be a happy experience for boys. If we adopt a more strictly medical perspective of psychotherapy, we might be led to believe that therapy is only a means to an end. However, simply attending therapy appointments is itself therapeutic in that it establishes a form of commitment, accountability, and follow-through, which add mightily to a sense of autonomy and strength. It's true that many boys begin therapy reluctantly. Yet if therapy is effective at connecting with a boy's sense of interest and purpose, it doesn't take long for the therapy to become a more satisfying experience. This doesn't mean avoiding values of being practical and task-focused. Usually, it's practical and relieving to boys to convert behavioral or emotional problems into a specific task. Quite often, this means breaking a challenge down into a set of steps that can be enacted over time.

In many cases, it is crucial that older boys feel a strong sense of acceptance and belief. There is no substitute for being relentlessly positive, which includes projecting interest and respect. When therapy gets off track, as in those times when it seems unclear who's driving the agenda for treatment, it's helpful to constructively assert that *the ultimate purpose of treatment is to have the best, most enjoyable life possible.* This is my steadfast belief. When this larger life goal is at the center of treatment, a powerful bond develops.

Checking in with parents

A key question in most cases is how often to meet with parents. Generally, the initial meeting is done with parents and child. Other members of the family can be included at any time it would be beneficial. As a rule, I believe it's important for boys to develop a sense of themselves apart from parents. This separation, even for younger boys, is how they become themselves, including speaking frankly, and trying on different perspectives. Therapy is a place of practice and experimentation. Most boys don't have a lot of experience in therapy, so it's a unique opportunity for them to shape their individual voices. Still, it's good practice to invite parents to note any current concerns at the start of the session, or by email. When the situation warrants, it's also good practice to invite parents into a session at the end to update them on important developments, or to answer questions related to the goals of therapy. These rules of thumb are of course superseded when dramatic content emerges that requires a parent's inclusion, or when some type of authority must be notified. In my own practice, such situations are extremely rare. Often, when I want to meet with parents, the meeting is accomplished as a separate session so that a boy's therapy time is not shortened. This also provides an opportunity to have a franker conversation with parents than I would in the presence of their child. This is not an attempt to be secretive, but there are times when it is necessary to advocate for boys in a neutral space where adult emotions don't become an additional worry, or bad memory.

Neurobiology of ADHD

It might seem unusual to be addressing a specific diagnostic concern in this mostly general chapter on therapy with boys. However, we live in a time where the prevalence of ADHD (better understood as executive dysfunction) is so great and is so often a relevant aspect of a boy's clinical picture, that it warrants special examination. It's helpful to begin with some basic information about the prefrontal cortex of the brain, and related elements of executive function. In my previous book, *No Mind Left Behind: Understanding and Fostering Executive Control — The Eight Essential Brain Skills Every Child Needs to Thrive,* I explained eight pillars of executive function in detail: Initiation, Attention, Cognitive Flexibility, Working Memory, Organization, Planning, Self-Monitoring, Emotional Control.[7] My purpose in writing *No Mind Left Behind* was to help families and schools get beyond a tendency to moralize about troublesome work habits that have less to do with character and effort than brain dysfunction. It's reassuring for boys to understand the basic brain mechanics of these habits as well. However, it's also necessary to relate this information in terms that make sense to the child, according to his age. For younger boys, I often compare the brain to a spaceship, with the prefrontal cortex being the command and control center. We talk about what would happen if the captain of the spaceship fell asleep, which is like what happens in a brain where the prefrontal cortex is understimulated. Older boys can handle a more scientific explanation of the process, which is greatly aided by a brain model, always kept within reach. The gist of this explanation is that a person's brain may be working against his best intentions — through no fault of his own.

No Mind Left Behind discusses *options of first resort* for executive dysfunction in detail. It is essential that an accurate assessment of executive functions be made so that interventions can be applied accordingly. We do not live in the age of one-size-fits-all ADHD. Although the term ADHD has become commonly recognized by virtually everyone, the term itself is unfortunately too simplistic. Thinking in terms of executive functions does much more to differentiate distinct dimensions of this prevalent syndrome.

There are times when a referral for medication needs to be made which might involve a pediatrician, primary care physician, psychiatrist, psychiatric nurse, or neurologist. When the issue appears to be primarily a need for psychostimulant medication, it's often most expeditious to refer a child to a pediatrician or primary care physician. When the clinical picture is more complex, and it looks as though more than one medication might be needed, it's better to refer to a child psychiatrist. In all cases, it is good practice to send a letter to the prescribing physician outlining what has been observed about the child's mental status, and assuring the physician that the child's mental status will be continually assessed through ongoing treatment. Significant changes in mental status should be communicated promptly. Professional communication does much to establish a close alliance with allied providers and is very reassuring to parents, who understandably want all providers to share critical information.

School Consultations

Because school is a primary community for children, it may be necessary to work on improving a child's adjustment in that community. School consultations might address academic issues, behavioral problems, or emotional dysregulation. These meetings are an excellent opportunity to advocate for boys and the kinds of instructional strategies that work well for them. It's important to remain positive at school consultations because school staff are often feeling sensitive and judged. Particularly where discussion revolves around boys who have learning problems, and where teachers have been somewhat unsuccessful, there is a strong inclination to point fingers and to want to be validated. Therapists feel the same sensitivity around behavioral problems. Sometimes advocacy involves helping a boy to get an IEP done, while at other times discussing the limitations of an IEP could be involved.

Although schools often suggest psychoeducational testing, these evaluations have shortfalls. Specifically, the recommendations tend to be somewhat generic. It's great to learn everything one can about a boy's processing differences and learning style, but a useful evaluation is not an abstract assessment done purely in the interest of greater knowledge. These evaluations ought to have real implications, and should point the way toward improving the situation. Recommendations should address instructional changes and other environmental considerations, as well as work habits and study skills for the child in question.

Because of processing differences, boys often have inclinations that are at odds with the tone and tempo of the school day.

For many boys, the daily ritual of school is an exercise in swimming upstream. In the interest of meeting situational demands for compliance and performance, schools risk ignoring what is subjectively important to students. This has devastating consequences for boys, schools, and our civilization.

We are long past the time when we can dictate to boys in an authoritarian manner what is important for them to learn. Engaging boys means creating relevant experiences. In my view, school consultations are a place where we seek a higher level of congruity between what feels right and interesting to students, and what takes place during the school day.

Honor

Cracking the Boy Code began with a discussion of the power of a specific mantra: *strength and honor*. This chapter will conclude by reinforcing the power of honor as a central theme in the psychotherapy of boys. We've examined the importance of bringing a degree of seriousness and gravity to our interactions with boys, and no idea seems to do that as effectively as the concept of honor. To speak openly and matter-of-factly about the value of honor, and where it comes from, has a galvanizing effect on boys' consciousness. Even the most disaffected boys seem to have a peripheral awareness that honor is something important to acquire. Despite that awareness, honor remains vague for most. And in that vagueness honor is elusive and abstract. For most, there is no plan. Therapy is a good place to connect "want" with "plan." Specifically, helping boys to understand what actions are honorable, and why.

This is not a mandate for speeches or moralizing in psychotherapy. I'm not a believer in hammering on the issue of honor session after session, or even for more than a few minutes at a time. But its reference early on in treatment. and as a recurring concept throughout treatment, is a powerful assertion that psychotherapy is a journey toward strength, responsibility, and goodness.

These concepts are not exclusively relevant to boys. We all benefit from working toward an honorable life. In *Cracking the Boy Code*, I have focused on key developmental themes in boys' lives, and what I have learned about their psychology. Therapy with boys has been my primary laboratory for experimenting with strategies for helping, and for the recommendations made in this book. Without experimentation, psychotherapy eventually loses its momentum and sense of possibility.

The joy of discussing honor with so many kinds of boys, of different ages, is that its form is never quite the same. How it becomes manifest in the lives of each person is organic and individual, but always powerful. My plea here is not for a slogan or "honor commercial," but for an authentic invocation of a spirit of honor. This is the true character of courage and possibility, of resilience and momentum. These attributes are the deep form of a life well lived, and what we should hope for every boy.

Remember

- Relationship is what powers therapy forward. Find a therapist with an instinct for relationship. This triumphs over theories, rules, and professional status.
- Activity-based therapy works well to engage younger boys. Older boys seek consequential conversation. It's not reasonable to expect boys and young men to embrace hours of discussion around their bad habits. The best therapy moves toward something, rather than away from something.
- Emphasizing some aspects of agency — doing and accomplishing things — is more fundamental than insight or reflecting on emotions. It is the key to engagement.

Points to Consider

- You may have to interview several therapists to find the right one.
- Allow boys some privacy about the content of sessions, especially as they get older.
- Relationship-based treatment becomes more effective over time, as trust and rapport increase.

Appendix: Fifty Purposeful Work Ideas

THESE IDEAS PROVIDE STARTING POINTS FOR DISCUSSION. Please don't be limited by them. The task of sorting out a project, figuring out logistics, and finding good supervision are all part of the process. The single most important factor in generating success is understanding *that purposeful work for young people most often needs supervision by someone who is patient, and who is a good teacher.* Companionship and collaboration make work more fun, and more meaningful. Boys who participate in endeavors like those suggested below will learn something about a task, as well as something about themselves. Remember that the realm of purposeful activities is largely unknown to youth, yet proves to be far more interesting to them than either they or we might imagine.

1. Work in a community garden
2. Build a boat
3. Volunteer at an animal shelter
4. Begin a small service business, like yardwork or shoveling snow
5. Become an intern in an adult's business
6. Create a public service website
7. Improve school grounds
8. Learn to cook
9. Renovate a bedroom
10. Write a book, poetry collection, or script
11. Take and exhibit photographs
12. Help design a home improvement
13. Set up a computer for another family member or friend
14. Help coach younger children in your favorite sport
15. Be a fishing guide for younger children

16. Organize a camping outing with friends
17. Tutor a peer
18. Volunteer for a field study with a naturalists' group
19. Set up a table at a flea market
20. Start a small pet care business
21. Design a new game
22. Apprentice with a craftsperson
23. Create a mock investment portfolio
24. Fix something with a skillful adult
25. Be an audio/visual assistant at school
26. Organize a book drive for charity
27. Volunteer for a local or regional litter control project
28. Fix or maintain a local woodland trail
29. Start a podcast on an area of expertise
30. Create a YouTube channel
31. Build a Minecraft server, providing services to other players
32. Volunteer for Habitat for Humanity
33. Work for a political candidate
34. Start a business on eBay
35. Start an anime lending library
36. Repair a car or motorcycle
37. Build a robot
38. Get involved in blacksmithing
39. Build a fence
40. Learn how to make your own surfboard or skateboard
41. Fix a bicycle
42. Write movie or music reviews
43. Contribute photos to a local paper
44. Start a band
45. Manage social media for a nearby business
46. Begin a social media campaign for a good cause
47. Build a bench or picnic table
48. Be a museum guide or interpreter
49. Assume responsibility for a pet
50. Usher at a sporting event or theater

Endnotes

Prologue

1. Adam J. Cox. *Boys of Few Words: Raising Our Sons to Communicate and Connect.* Guilford Press, 2005.

Part I

1. Peter Salovey and John D. Mayer. "Emotional intelligence." *Imagination, Cognition and Personality* 9, no. 3 (1990): 185–211.
2. Barbara B. Sherwin. "Estrogenic effects on memory in women." *Annals of the New York Academy of Sciences* 743, no. 1 (1994): 213–230. doi: 10.1111/j.1749-6632.1994.tb55794.x.
3. Vincent J. Schmithorst, Scott K. Holland, and Bernard J. Dardzinski. "Developmental differences in white matter architecture between boys and girls." *Human Brain Mapping* 29 (2008): 696–710. doi:10.1002/hbm.20431.
4. Doreen Kimura. *Sex and Cognition.* MIT Press, 1990.
5. John Medina. *Brain Rules: 12 Principles for Surviving and Thriving at Work, Home, and School,* 2nd ed. Pear Press, 2014.
6. Sherwin. "Estrogenic effects on memory in women."
7. Annett Schirmer, A., Sonja A. Kotz, and Angela D. Friederici. "Sex differentiates the role of emotional prosody during word processing." *Cognitive Brain Research* 14, no. 2 (August 2002): 228–233. dx.doi.org/10.1016/S0926-6410(02)00108-8.
8. Walter R. Boot, Daniel P. Blakely, and Daniel J. Simons. "Do action video games improve perception and cognition?" *Frontiers in Psychology* 13 (2011). doi.org/10.3389/fpsyg.2011.00226.
9. Jane M. Healy. *Endangered Minds. Why Children Don't Think and What We Can Do About It.* Simon & Schuster, 1999.

10. Adam J. Cox. "The case for boredom: Stimulation, Civility, and Modern Boyhood." *New Atlantis* 27 (Spring 2010): 122–125. thenewatlantis.com/publications/the-case-for-boredom.
11. Harold Mosak and Michael Maniacci. *Primer of Adlerian Psychology: The Analytic-Behavioural-Cognitive Psychology of Alfred Adler.* Routledge, 1999.

Part II
1. "Encourage your boy." *West Side News* Vol. 7, no. 1 (April 20, 1889): 1. corescholar.libraries.wright.edu/cgi/viewcontent.cgi?article=1006 &context=west_side_news.
2. Alain De Botton. *The Pleasures and Sorrows of Work.* Vintage, 2010: 80.
3. Matthew B. Crawford. *Shop Class as Soulcraft: An Inquiry into the Value of Work.* Penguin, 2009: 15.
4. Adam J. Cox. "Locating Significance in the Lives of Boys." Qualitative research commissioned by International Boys' Schools Coalition, 2011. theibsc.org/teaching-learning/global-research/reports.
5. Doug Stowe. "Back to school, the wisdom of the hands." *Woodcraft Magazine* Issue 6 (October-November 2005): 68–71. woodcraft. com/products/woodcraft-magazine-downloadable-issue-6-october-november-2005.
6. Matthew B. Crawford. *The World Beyond Your Head: On Becoming an Individual in an Age of Distraction.* Farrar, Straus & Giroux, 2015: 253–254.
7. Adam J. Cox. *No Mind Left Behind: Understanding and Fostering Executive Control — The Eight Essential Brain Skills Every Child Needs to Thrive.* Perigee, 2007.

Acknowledgments

OVER THE FOUR YEARS DURING WHICH THIS BOOK WAS WRITTEN, many have shared their stories and advice. I thank my professional colleagues for their interest in and enthusiasm for this project, and for the opportunities they have afforded me to work with boys at a great many schools and community settings. I am especially grateful to the International Boys' Schools Coalition (IBSC) who took an early interest in my work, giving me the opportunity to conduct a global study of boys among their member schools. There are many in the IBSC whose ideas and support have been critical, and I am particularly appreciative of Brad Adams, David Armstrong, John Botti, Jim Power, Mary Gauthier, and Brian Lee. In Australia, at the Shore School in Sydney, I give thanks to Headmaster Tim Wright, and former Housemaster David Anderson, who welcomed me for a brief stint as a visiting scholar, working on issues of adolescent passage and the meaning of masculinity.

My wife Jacquelyne, and son Addison, have been steadfast supporters, always willing to read the manuscript and offer valuable insights. How fortunate to have these contributions as a check on my own perspectives. Most of what I've learned has come from direct interaction with boys. Their willingness to be open, and to engage in civil conversation, has connected me with a psychology far more complex than what I knew years ago. Through all the moments of tension, debate with parents and schools, the struggle for achievement, coping with loss, the frontier of social anxiety, the tsunami of electronica, and the irritation of trying to belong to a world where options for enduring happiness and purpose are presently too limited, we have continued to talk. A thousand *thank-you's* for this. I have aimed to be worthy of your trust.

Index

About the Author

A DAM COX IS A CLINICAL PSYCHOLOGIST, author, speaker, and educational consultant. A frequent lecturer on the emotional and cognitive development of youth, Adam was commissioned by the International Boys' Schools Coalition to conduct a global school-based research project, *Locating Significance in the Lives of Boys,* in which he investigated how boys find authentic meaning and purpose in their lives. He interviewed students and teachers from a wide variety of social and educational backgrounds in the US, Canada, UK, Singapore, South Africa, New Zealand, and Australia.

Dr. Cox has developed experiential education and advisory programs in the US and abroad aimed at building diverse forms of capability among youth. The author of the first book on executive functions for a lay audience, Dr. Cox created the Eight Pillar model of executive functioning which has been widely adopted by schools and educational organizations.

Dr. Cox is the author of *On Purpose Before Twenty* (designated one of the "Best Courageous Books of 2014" by Parker Palmer's Center for Courage and Renewal); *No Mind Left Behind: Understanding and Fostering Executive Control — The Eight Essential Brain Skills Every Child Needs to Thrive* and *Boys of Few Words: Raising Our Sons to Communicate and Connect.* He writes a newsletter called "Family Matters" at DrAdamCox.com.

A Note about the Publisher

New Society Publishers is an activist, solutions-oriented publisher focused on publishing books for a world of change. Our books offer tips, tools, and insights from leading experts in sustainable building, homesteading, climate change, environment, conscientious commerce, renewable energy, and more — positive solutions for troubled times.

We're proud to hold to the highest environmental and social standards of any publisher in North America. This is why some of our books might cost a little more. We think it's worth it!

- We print all our books in North America, never overseas
- All our books are printed on **100% post-consumer recycled paper**, processed chlorine free, with low-VOC vegetable-based inks (since 2002)
- Our corporate structure is an innovative employee shareholder agreement, so we're one-third employee-owned (since 2015)
- We're carbon-neutral (since 2006)
- We're certified as a B Corporation (since 2016)

At New Society Publishers, we care deeply about *what* we publish — but also about *how* we do business.

Download our catalogue at https://newsociety.com/Our-Catalog or for a printed copy please email info@newsocietypub.com or call 1-800-567-6772 ext 111

New Society Publishers
ENVIRONMENTAL BENEFITS STATEMENT

For every 5,000 books printed, New Society saves the following resources:[1]

17	Trees
1,495	Pounds of Solid Waste
1,645	Gallons of Water
2,145	Kilowatt Hours of Electricity
2,717	Pounds of Greenhouse Gases
12	Pounds of HAPs, VOCs, and AOX Combined
4	Cubic Yards of Landfill Space

[1]Environmental benefits are calculated based on research done by the Environmental Defense Fund and other members of the Paper Task Force who study the environmental impacts of the paper industry.